THE Fighter's MINDSET

The Fighter's Mindset
Transform Adversity Into Your Ally

Melissa Mae Jordy

Published by Game Changer Publishing

Paperback ISBN: 979-8-90158-068-4
Hardcover ISBN: 979-8-90158-069-1
Digital ISBN: 979-8-90158-070-7

www.GameChangerPublishing.com

Advance Praise

"Melissa Mae Jordy is energy personified. And fresh energy is what many of us need in a time like this. If you're needing a burst of inspiration, she's written a book that can help you stand back up."

— Daniel Grothe, Pastor and author

"The Fighter's Mindset is a powerful reminder that adversity is not here to break us, but to prepare us. Melissa Mae Jordy transforms real pain, faith, and hard-earned lessons into a practical framework for anyone ready to rise with intention instead of reacting with fear. This book matters because it doesn't just inspire hope; it teaches you how to stand back up, anchored in purpose, and fight forward with meaning."

— David Meltzer, Speaker, Author, Entrepreneur

"The fighter's mindset is a must for anyone who wants to win this fight we call life. The practical insights and strategies from someone who knows how to keep getting up are priceless."

— Douglas Weiss, Ph.D., Psychologist and author

Dedication

To my children, Katia, Elyas, and Jordyn.
You have strengthened my walk and shaped my growth in ways that changed me forever.
You've reminded me that our stories are part of something far bigger than this moment.

My hope is that your lives always reach beyond the temporary,
rooted in truth, anchored in purpose,
and aligned with what lasts for eternity

Read This First

As a thank you for buying this book, I'd love to connect!

Scan the QR Code:

THE Fighter's MINDSET

TRANSFORM ADVERSITY INTO YOUR ALLY

Melissa Mae Jordy

Table of Contents

FOREWORD

By David Meltzer

Life is a battlefield, filled with challenges that test our strength, resilience, and purpose. As you open Melissa Mae Jordy's *The Fighter's Mindset,* you might wonder why I, David Meltzer, have chosen to write this foreword.

I may not have fought on a physical battlefield, but I've faced my share of battles, both personal and professional. And through each one, I've learned that success and happiness are forged not in the absence of adversity but in how we respond to it. Melissa's journey epitomizes this truth, and her story has inspired me in ways I'm excited to share with you. When I met Melissa, it felt like stepping onto a battlefield of life together. She had already endured more than her fair share of hardships, yet she faced it all with an undeniable grit and determination. That's what makes her a fighter, and that's what makes this book a game-changer for anyone navigating their own battles.

What sets *The Fighter's Mindset* apart is its unwavering focus on empowering you to transform adversity into strength. Life isn't about avoiding battles; it's about how you fight them and, more importantly, who you become in the process. Melissa introduces the FIGHT concept, starting with "Foundation," a principle I resonate with deeply.

In my life, I've come to understand that a strong foundation doesn't guarantee smooth sailing, but it does ensure a safe landing. Melissa's approach will guide you to build that foundation, allowing you to stand firm when the storms of life hit. She provides the tools and strategies you need to face challenges head-on and emerge stronger on the other side.

My mission is to empower over 1 billion people to be happy, and I firmly believe this book will serve as a catalyst for that mission. Melissa's authenticity, courage, and ability to inspire are unparalleled. She's not just a fighter. She's a guide, a mentor, and an embodiment of the mindset this world needs.

As you read this book, let Melissa's story inspire you to uncover your own fighter's mindset. She'll be right there in your corner, coaching you to dig deep, hold strong, and transform your greatest challenges into your greatest triumphs.

You've got this. And with Melissa's wisdom and guidance, you're not just prepared for the fight. You're poised to win.

—**David Meltzer** is a renowned sports executive with 2,064,000 followers across six social media platforms. He is the host and executive producer of the Apple TV series *2 Minute Drill* and *Office Hours*. He is also the host and EP of Entrepreneur TV Network's number one business show, *Elevator Pitch*. David is featured in many books, movies, and TV shows, including *World's Greatest Motivators, Think and Grow Rich,* and *Beyond the Secret,* which aired on Netflix. His former role as CEO of the legendary

Leigh Steinberg Entertainment Agency inspired the movie *Jerry Maguire* starring Tom Cruise. He is a three-time international bestselling author and one of the world's top entrepreneurs, investors, and business coaches. www.dmeltzer.com

ABOUT THE AUTHOR

Melissa Mae's journey is not just one of overcoming adversity; it's a fierce transformation, taking life's hardest punches and turning them into stepping stones. The early battles she fought shaped her into the woman she is today: a force of nature, driven by purpose, faith, and a desire to serve and uplift others.

Raised in poverty by a single mother, Melissa learned early on that life doesn't hand out anything for free. Every day was a fight for survival, and success was never guaranteed. But through it all, Melissa never allowed her circumstances to define her. She realized that the foundation of true success wasn't in the things she had or didn't have. It was in her attitude, her choices, and her relentless drive to rise above obstacles and hardships.

A pivotal moment for her was joining the U.S. Air Force, a decision born of necessity but also a deep desire to prove to herself and to the world that she was capable of something much more than average. The military taught her discipline, resilience, and the importance of mental toughness. But more than that, it instilled in her a deep sense of purpose. It wasn't just about serving her country; it was also about serving herself, taking ownership of her life, and creating a future that was not dictated by the limitations of her past.

Melissa's time in the Air Force not only honed her skills as a fighter but also shaped her into a leader. The military's emphasis on "teamwork and service above self" became a core principle she carried with her long after her departure. It was here that she learned the value of selflessness, the power of showing up for others, and the incredible strength that comes from working toward something bigger than yourself.

But as her journey shifted to civilian life, the challenges didn't disappear. If anything, they became more complex. She faced painful personal losses, failed marriages, and abusive relationships, each one a reminder that life is messy, unpredictable, and often cruel. However, rather than succumbing to these struggles, Melissa chose to face them head-on. She learned to turn every setback into a setup for something greater. Each failure became a lesson, and each heartbreak became a springboard to greater personal growth.

The transition from military service to civilian entrepreneurship was not an easy one, but it was a natural evolution for someone like Melissa, who thrives in environments where others might flounder. Her resilience found a new outlet in the business world. As a serial entrepreneur, she began building businesses that reflected her core values of service, authenticity, and empowerment. She became a high-performance coach, using her own story as a testament to what's possible when you refuse to let the world dictate your worth.

Melissa has a strong background in both fitness and combat sports. With over eight years of competing in fitness competitions, reaching national levels, she gained invaluable experience in discipline, mental toughness, and overcoming challenges. Her journey in fitness helped her develop a deep understanding of the importance of mental resilience in achieving physical goals. For the last six years, Melissa has also trained fighters in boxing and kickboxing. Through this, she honed her ability to instill not only physical strength but also the mental toughness required to excel in combat sports. Her diverse experiences make her a well-rounded mentor capable of guiding others to achieve both physical and mental growth.

As a speaker, author, and coach, Melissa now dedicates her life to helping others tap into their own inner strength. She believes that every person has a fighter within, and it's just a matter of unlocking that potential. Through her teachings, she empowers individuals to step into the "ring of life" with confidence, resilience, and a mindset that no obstacle is too big to overcome.

One of the cornerstones of Melissa's philosophy is that true strength comes from being rooted in something deeper than yourself. Her unshakable faith in God and her understanding of His promises give her the courage to keep going when the odds are stacked against her. She doesn't view herself as a victim of her circumstances; she sees herself as a warrior, armed with purpose and guided by a Higher Power.

Through it all, Melissa remains committed to living as her authentic self: a woman who embraces both her strengths and vulnerabilities. She's a fighter, but she's also a servant leader, always looking for ways to give back and lift others as she climbs. She's an athlete, pushing herself physically and mentally to always be at her best. And, above all, she's a mother, fiercely dedicated to shaping the next generation with the same values of resilience, faith, and self-belief that have guided her own journey.

Her life exemplifies what's possible when you refuse to give up. It's a testament to the power of resilience, the importance of staying grounded in your purpose, and the transformative power of faith. Melissa Mae's story is one of strength, growth, and unrelenting faith that, no matter how tough the battle, the promise of victory is always within reach for those who are willing to fight for it.

Introduction

BEFORE THE BELL RINGS

"I have fought the good fight,
I have finished the race,
I have kept the faith."
–2 Timothy 4:7 (NIV)

In 2004, the air was thick with heat and dust the day I stepped off the aircraft in Iraq. I still remember the moment: how the sun hung low over the desert, how the ground felt foreign beneath my boots. I was a young airman, trained but untested, full of adrenaline and uncertainty.

Then it happened.

The siren pierced our ears: "Code Red! Code Red!" For a split second, I froze. At first, I thought it was a drill until I saw the urgency in our leaders' faces, their voices sharp and commanding: "Move! Move! Move!" Immediately, the sound of boots pounding the tarmac echoed all around me as we ran toward the bunkers. My heart was racing, my senses locked in.

That was the day I realized tomorrow isn't guaranteed. That day marked me. It was the moment I understood what it means to live prepared and to treat every breath like borrowed time. That is what fighters do. We stay ready. We live like it's our last round.

Looking back, I now see that fighting Iraq wasn't just about physical survival. It was training for a deeper kind of battle, the one that happens in the mind and spirit. Because the truth is, your fight doesn't end when you hang up the uniform or leave the field. Life has its own battlegrounds: business, relationships, grief, purpose, and faith. And just like in combat, the difference between panic and power is preparation. As a fighter, I learned to move from reaction to readiness. As a coach, entrepreneur, and speaker, I now help others do the same.

You may not be in a war zone, but you've likely faced your own "Code Red." Maybe it was a diagnosis, a betrayal, a loss, or a moment of doubt. Maybe you've been hit by something that shook your faith or made you question your strength. I get it. I've been there too. But here's the truth I learned in the desert and in every storm since: You are built for this.

You were never meant to live in defeat. You were created to fight with faith.

The Fighter's Mindset

This book isn't about avoiding pain or pretending your battle doesn't exist. It's about transforming adversity into your ally, using every hit, setback, and trial as a stepping stone toward your purpose. Through the FIGHT Framework, I'll show you how to develop the stance, systems, and spiritual strength to keep moving forward when life throws its hardest punches.

Here's your corner strategy:

- **F** – Foundation of Faith: Build on the Rock that cannot be moved.
- **I** – Ignite the Fighter Within: Fear is a signal, not a sentence. Light your flame and fight with purpose.
- **G** – Get to Work: Action alleviates anxiety. Stack small wins. Move with intention.
- **H** – Hand Set, Heart Set, Head Set: Stay aligned with your purpose and values. Don't fight battles that aren't yours.
- **T** – Time to Reflect: Every round has a lesson. Learn from it. Celebrate the wins. Refine the strategy.

This is how fighters grow, not by avoiding the hit, but by learning to move through it with grace, grit, and God.

Corner Drill: Your Fighter Name and Calling

Every great fighter carries a name into battle. It's more than a title; it's identity, intention, and anointed purpose.

I go by the fighter name "Heaven's Haymaker" because my strength doesn't come from me; it comes from above. My fight is rooted in faith, and my mission is to lead others to their own divine inner strength. When I step into the ring of life, I'm not just throwing punches; I'm training champions, building warriors of faith, and leading others to discover the same resilience that saved me.

Now it's your turn.

Your fighter name will be the identity you choose to embody when life presses in. It's who you will become when fear whispers, and you answer back with faith. It's the warrior, the fighter, and the champion inside you who refuses to quit.

Take a few moments and claim yours:

My Fighter Name: ______________________________

When you declare your fighter name, you're not just identifying who you are. You're aligning with the fighter within. You're stepping into your calling and are prepared for purpose.

Your fight is your testimony. Every scar, every victory, every time you rise again, you're showing others how to stand strong in theirs. You're making an impact.

So before the bell rings, take a breath. Set your stance.

Remember who you are and why you're here.

You're not just in the fight.

You are the fighter.

And this is where your comeback begins.

Round 1

SUCKER PUNCH

"Getting knocked down is a given. Getting up and moving forward is a choice."
–Zig Ziglar

Sucker punches, true to the name, come out of nowhere. They suck, big time! Whether it's in the gut or to the face, the intent is to take you out. No mercy. Just a brutal shot determined to lay you flat on your back and put you out cold.

As a fighter, you will, without question or hesitation, get hit, and at times those hits come in the form of a sucker punch. This is a guarantee. When you put yourself in the ring or on the battlefield, when you decide to "go to war" against someone or something, taking damage is just the name of the game. As an entrepreneur, athlete, and/or high-performer, not just existing but living life to its fullest, you're asking to get hit. It's just the way the game is played. However, the way you choose to *respond* to these battle wounds will determine your destiny.

Sucker punches and hits come in all shapes and sizes. You might be experiencing one right now, whether it's a breakup, a divorce, or a disagreement in your relationship with your partner. Chances are that you have a child or children, and you may be treading through the perils of parenthood. Your professional environment could have you questioning life choices, and you're dreading getting up in the morning.

- Were you fired from a job?
- Do you need to "fire" someone in your life?
- Did life unexpectedly take someone special from you without warning?
- Were you or a family member diagnosed with a disease that has you on your knees, asking why?
- Has a project or business that you've poured your entire world into just gone up in flames or flooded you with debt?
- Has a vision of becoming an athlete been ripped from you due to injury or accident?

This list could continue for pages. Go ahead and add yours here:

____?

Sucker punches are always unexpected. Taking damage while in the ring is going to happen. I am no stranger to this danger, and I have taken my fair share of hits just like you have. This is our reality. As fighters, we ask to be placed in the ring. As warriors, we signed up for battle. We decided to fight. We're the "chosen ones," geared up and ready to go to war (literally or figuratively). We willingly sign our name on the dotted line, asking the universe to test us. Unlike the draft, where it's mandatory that you enroll and fight regardless of the suck factor, you have voluntarily signed your name on the dotted line and said, "I'll fight for what I believe in."

You may not understand this completely right now. Why would anyone voluntarily embrace the suck and place themselves in a fight? As the chapters progress, your understanding of what it means to be a champion fighter or an entrepreneur at the top of your game or a high performer, and why we willingly go to battle, will make much more sense.

Stay with me.

You may be an amateur fighter entering the ring for the first time. I applaud your courage. This decision to fulfill your destiny takes gumption and faith. You have chosen to be one of the few who refuse to live a life of mediocrity.

You could be a seasoned fighter reading this. As an experienced fighter myself, I stand and applaud you. You have already embraced the suck and continue to make the decision to fight, knowing this is not the easy path that much of the population continues to choose. As a skilled fighter, you have set your focus on becoming a champion. There is this lingering feeling that there is more out there for you. That you haven't reached your full potential. The following chapters will add powerful tools to your toolkit to assist you in achieving exactly that.

Take a moment and visualize the last time you were "sucker punched." The pain may seem just as real right now. A fog of confusion surrounds you. Your heart could be aching. Your ego is bruised. Your eyes are swelling from tears. The pain is so damn real. The disappointment looks back at you in the mirror. Your heart rate speeds up, and your body becomes uneasy recalling the details. Sick to your stomach, you find it difficult to get out of bed. Sucker punches SUCK. Hunched over, you fall to your knees and utter, "Why me? What did I do to deserve this?"

The questions continue to race through your head. Doubt, insecurity, embarrassment. You start questioning your faith, your strength, your purpose (if you even know what that is), and your ability to get back up.

Getting hit hurts in more ways than one.

Getting sucker punched can literally take the life out of you. Like a squall on a sunny day, storm clouds blanket your world. The winds are strong, the fog disrupts your sight, and you're left in a state of high alert. The radio urges you to take shelter. Your phone is beeping with notifications of what's to come. The desire to return to your comfort zone, where it's safe, races through your mind, seeming like the best choice, the easy option. And honestly, that's what the majority will choose: to freeze or to take flight.

A sucker punch is a storm of catastrophic proportions; your world feels like it's ending. It's the perfect storm, and others would completely understand if you chose to return to comfort and the status quo, to "follow the sheep" and settle, and to take shelter in a land of mediocrity. The pull is strong.

Your hope is diminishing, your heart is aching, and you're mentally, physically, and emotionally drained. It may seem like you have been fighting on a battlefield of desolation for what feels like forever. You start to beg for the round to be called. You desperately want the pain to stop.

You're at a point where you must make a decision. You can stay where you're at and lose the round by submission. Let that bell ring, and watch as the referee raises the hand of your opponent.

Or, despite the damage, warnings, and chaos happening around you, you can choose to listen to the little voice inside your head that reminds you you're a fighter. That you must get up. That your destiny is on the other side of this storm. That there is indeed a calm after the storm. That you must fight. Retreat is not on the table.

Compounded over time, these sucker punches, hits, self-inflicted challenges, or life's unexpected knockouts have a way of taking a toll on even the most competent fighters. You're human. Part of becoming a champion, making it to the top and grabbing that title, winning the battle, requires that you continue to train yourself and equip yourself with the necessary tools to fight your battles.

Conversely, not knowing how to navigate through these challenges after getting hit or sucker punched will leave you crumpled on the ground, falling back into unhealthy patterns, bad habits, vices, or raising the white flag and sadly throwing in the towel, giving up. The ripple effect this has on your life keeps you from reaching your true potential of champion status and fulfilling your destiny.

Like any champion who has weathered the storm, so can you. The following chapters will equip you with the offensive and defensive techniques you need to rise and defeat limiting beliefs and a scarcity mindset.

I am no stranger to challenges, knockouts, and storms. Honestly, I feel as if God has placed his hand on top of my fragile head and said, "My dear, you will face a multitude of challenges." Mind you, as you will notice later in this book, he also said, "My dear, you will overcome and conquer these challenges, because you're a fighter." I was, however, hard of hearing at times.

REMINDER: We'll keep going through the same challenges, experiencing similar pains and storms until we finally learn the lesson.

No one is excluded from the experience of facing challenges, storms, and sucker punches. In fact, those of us with a high calling will find that we have more ring time. Those who have accepted the journey to become a champion will find themselves living on a battlefield. This should not scare you, but excite you. You're destined for greatness. You have been appointed by a Bigger Source to have a massive impact during your time on this planet.

Hello, Chosen One.

Knocked Out

The last words my mother uttered to me were, "I love you." Out of nowhere, right to the kidney, this was the punch that left me barely able to breathe. I curled over only to take a roundhouse kick to the face. Knocked out. Put to sleep. I lay in a pool of my own blood in the ring, curled up in the fetal position. Over the phone, in another state, from a hospital bed, Mom was out of my reach. "My head hurts so bad, I love you," she uttered. I knew something wasn't right, so I begged her to get the nurse's attention.

"Mom, I love you. Please let me talk to the nurse." This was pain I'd never experienced before. I had faced an opponent advanced far beyond my years, an enemy no one should have to cross paths with.

* * *

I grew up in a single-parent household where my mom and I were a team. My dad was absent from my life, and the only consistent father figures I can recall growing up with were my step-sister's father briefly and my step-brother's father. Dad had chosen another lifestyle that included gambling. He gambled away our belongings and even my mom, and subsequently our family. He moved to California from the "biggest little city" of Reno, Nevada, to start a new life. Mom, my older brother, and I remained in Reno, where soon my other two siblings joined our family.

We looked after each other. There were four of us total. I was second in line, with my older brother just 18 months ahead of me and two younger siblings. Mom worked full-time, so it was a natural fit for me to look after the family while she earned a living for us. I tended to the home, completing chores, making dinners, and looking after my siblings while she was at work. I knew no different.

After graduating from high school, I left home to join the military. I had already signed up during my junior year. I was just seventeen, but the United States Air Force permitted the Delayed Entry Program. I marched into my senior year knowing I had a plan that would pay for college and put an end to a generational curse. This feeling of confidence was evident in my actions throughout my last year of high school.

But the burning desire to take care of and provide for my mother and family did not change. This was the driving force, the "why" that woke me up in the morning, and my mission.

* * *

I felt helpless in this situation, miles away from my mother, begging for the nurse's attention. I called the hospital relentlessly to finally be greeted by a nurse on the other line with my worst nightmare: My mom, my rock, was in a coma.

It wasn't until hours later that I received the details about Mom's "headache." She had checked into the hospital for a routine back surgery. After the operation, she'd been given medication to help with the pain. But the medication the hospital administered reacted adversely with another medication she was on. That led to the headache and ultimately to her going brain-dead.

In disbelief, my husband, whom I'll refer to as "Nick," and I packed up our two children and headed to Utah to find out what happened. Upon entering the hospital, it felt like I was in another world. I was hoping to wake up and find out this was all just a horrible dream. There was no way this could be real life. Mom was just 48. I talked to her just two days ago.

Confusion and heartache ran deep through my mind and body as I walked into her hospital room. I stared in disbelief at my mom in the hospital bed, kept alive only by a machine. I fell to my knees with my arms grasping toward her. Begging God to please let her wake up, tears pouring from my eyes. *This is not fair! We're not done yet!*

I stood there in front of Mother's lifeless body with one last question for me to answer:

Do I let them turn off the machine that's keeping my mother alive in a vegetative state?

It was one of the hardest decisions I've ever had to make. Standing there waiting for her to breathe on her own after. Seconds seemed like hours. My world stopped. The crowd went silent. The sound from the knockout could be heard across the arena.

My biggest driver in life, my "why," was to be able to provide for my mother, to finally give her a break from all the hard work and sacrifices she made for us. I wanted to take away her pain. I wanted to give her a better life. My fight against generational poverty, abuse, and violence was abruptly halted.

The bell rang before I could put in enough work to take her out of the fight. Life seemed so unfair. This was a hit I did not think I could recover from.

Have you ever felt that way? Like you wanted to give up? Like you could not get up? Have you been sucker punched so hard by this thing called life that all you want to do is curl up and disappear? This was one of those moments for me, one of the fights that many of us will find ourselves in, where the odds are stacked against us.

Confucius informed us, "Our greatest glory is not in never falling, but in rising every time we fall."

I was in my early twenties; I'd just given birth to my son, Elyas, six weeks prior to this debacle that I now replayed over and over in my mind.

My daughter, Katia, was four. Nick had just deployed overseas to Iraq with the USAF. My younger brother, William, fourteen years old, now had no mother or father. I was determined not to let them be casualties of this battle.

I had to get up. I had to wrap up my hands and prepare to get in the ring and fight for our family. There were no other options. No plan B. The mission, my "why," must be completed.

"Courage isn't having the strength to go on; it is going on when you don't have strength."
Napoleon Bonaparte

I packed up our belongings in Las Vegas and moved my family to Utah while my husband served in the Iraq War. The six months I spent there, handling my mother's affairs, would come to be one of the most difficult and challenging times I've ever experienced. I did my best to keep it together and raise my young children, surrounded by memories of my mom everywhere I turned. I missed her. I needed my husband. I felt deserted. I felt alone.

I would cry myself to sleep at night in such immense pain and heartache while the children slept. The days seemed long and unforgivable. "If only" consistently filled my thoughts. I was too late, and now I was paying the price.

It would not be for six long months before we'd return to a somewhat normal routine, if you could ever consider losing a parent "normal." In this case, that could not be any closer to the truth. My world shifted dramatically.

Going through such a traumatic experience without my support system or my husband by my side forced me to step into the ring and fight. It required that I find solutions to unimaginable challenges. I had to dig deep and find strength; had I not, I'd have been left dead on that battlefield next to my mom. I refused to allow there to be two casualties. I knew Mom would want me to rise up and fight, and so with what was left in me, I fought.

In the deep recesses of my mind, I'd hear Mom's voice. I attribute a lot of my ability to navigate this situation to her, through the examples she set for me as I grew up. Mom was a servant leader. She, like Jesus, loved without condition, served without expectancy, and gave without judgment.

She always put others before herself. From her example, I came to realize this situation could not be about me. My focus was on the mission, a skill I learned from my five years in the Air Force. My focus on the mission, coupled with servant leadership, became my solution. Impact and damage to my brother and children needed to be minimized. I'd been hand-selected for this mission; it was a position only I could fulfill. Welcome to Destiny.

When you put others as a priority despite your own feelings, somehow the difficult situations you face become easier to handle. I am not saying it was no big deal. What I'm saying is that a genuine desire to serve and not make it about you will help you take that next step in the most difficult of times. Even in situations where you can see no light at the end of the tunnel. As Les Brown said, "If you can look up, you can get up." Please, choose to get up and fight.

My husband and I ended up divorcing soon after Mother's passing and his return from Iraq. The impact of military deployment and family death proved too much for a young couple to navigate. I'll touch on this further later, but for now, just know that not allowing myself to grieve my mother's passing shaped my life in ways I carried for years.

My biggest lesson learned from that situation is this: *No one is guaranteed tomorrow. Hurry up and make today count.* That continues to be my mantra to this day. When I go to bed at night, it helps me to lay my head on my pillow knowing I did everything I could today to be the best version of me.

Blood, Sweat, and Tears

Are you in the middle of what seems like the fight of your life? Like the story I shared about my mother's passing, your fight feels like it's "going live" on ESPN. Amid what could be your last round, you picked up this book in hopes of finding a remedy for your pain. Blood, sweat, and tears have significant meaning to you. But your energy is depleted. You don't look like yourself or feel like yourself. While praying for reinforcements, this is not how you thought your life would play out.

"Man cannot make himself without suffering, for he is both the marble and the sculptor."
Alexis Carrel

This next story takes place about a year after Mother's passing. With my two small children in tow, I had been cruising along in a serious relationship for a few months. At first, everything seemed normal. But not just normal; it felt too good to be true. "Justin" was a successful small-business owner, and in the beginning, he seemed to care for me and my children.

The tide quickly turned soon after I agreed to move in with him. He immediately sought to control everything: my finances, my home, and any move I made that did not correspond with his way of thinking. It was easy to do, because Justin had convinced me that working for him was the best choice for our relationship and my career. A decent salary and a beautiful home were hard to say no to.

I did everything I could to please him, to no avail. He'd continually find fault with me. I was watched and felt "recorded." Every action was criticized if it didn't fall in line with his preferences. The independence and stability I thought I'd created for myself quickly got flipped upside down. I had been manipulated. My self-confidence had me questioning myself and giving credence to Justin's remarks: "You will never make it on your own." "If you try to leave, I'll make sure you never work again in this city." "I'll find you wherever you go." "You'll never be good enough for anyone else."

The need to provide for and survive for my family and not fail in another relationship kept me present in this war for far too long. Mean word after mean word, critical look upon critical look, I let him strip away my identity. I no longer recognized myself. All that was left was a set of dog tags inscribed with the name of an airman who existed only in the past. Now, buried deep in the grasp of this man's self-serving grip, hope diminished with each passing day. I had never felt so helpless. I had never felt so weak.

Have you ever found yourself in a similar situation where you felt completely helpless and hopeless? Tired, beat, and ready to give up? A battle so intense that the pain starts to become unbearable?

* * *

I remember it like it was yesterday. In June of 2010, in my son's room on the second floor of our home, Justin and I were in the midst of another one of our petty disagreements. This time was not like any of the others. Justin was infuriated that I had threatened to leave if he didn't calm down.

My body shook when Justin raised his voice, and his right hand formed a fist.

"If you don't do what I say, I'll…!" He glared at my son and walked in his direction. Elyas, just four at the time, stood there in confusion. The look on Elyas's face when he huddled in the corner sent my heart beating out of my chest. But like a lioness protecting her cub, I rushed forward, covering Elyas with my body.

Justin swung a fist and punched a hole in the wall right above our heads. Tears ran down my face in disbelief. I couldn't understand why a grown man would want to lay his hands on a woman, let alone a four-year-old boy.

"If I cannot have you, nobody can," Justin threatened, then stormed out of the room. To him, the hole meant he'd won. He got his message across, loud and clear.

But for me, that hole signified more than a warning. I knew this was the end of our relationship. I had to make a change immediately. This had to be the last round. Or the next round would result in a knockout for both my son and me.

Despite the challenges that lay ahead of me as a single mom, jobless, and without family in Las Vegas to help, I had to do whatever was necessary to escape this toxic environment. That was going to be the last punch Justin would throw at my children or me. The attempted assault triggered something lying dormant inside of me. It prompted the fighter within to rise up and take action. I may have lost the round, but I wasn't going to lose the fight. At my core, I am a fighter. I must fight. I began to rebuild.

It's incredible what happens when you *decide*: when you set your focus and attention on a goal, task, or a bigger vision, and combine that with intention, attention, and hard work. This gives the universe permission to grant you coincidences that align in favor of your choice. But you must make a move. Sitting or quitting isn't an option. But deciding that you will move forward in faith is.

The universe did just that for me. I was aligned with "Mark," a man whom I had met in a park behind our gated community, where our kids played together. Mark owned a moving company, and he assisted me with the move-out one weekend when Justin was out of town. Let's be honest, Mark was an angel.

Additionally, a tax refund check arrived at just the right time for me to put down a deposit and pay the first month's rent on a home a few miles from where we currently lived. Next, I interviewed for and landed a position at a college as an educational recruiter. This included a salary that would take care of the needs of me and my children. I want to say it was all coincidental, but in reality, I went from thinking I was being punished for my past to understanding that I was being protected and "promoted" to push forward to better things that God had in store for me.

I just had to decide to take *action*.

Mother's Day

Ironically, I am writing this chapter on Mother's Day. It's a holiday, as "Hallmark" as it may be, intended to celebrate a mother and all that she is and does for her children. Mother's Day to me is a day that confronts me head-on with sucker punches from the past. My mother's birthday falls in May, and since her passing, sometimes I still find it difficult to press forward without crying, thinking about what could have been. I am still healing. Because the wound is deep. The good ol' saying goes, "Time heals all wounds." Each year, it gets a little easier as I learn to change my narrative. And, as we'll discuss in depth in another chapter, time plus a perspective shift heals all wounds.

I also admitted my oldest daughter, "Kat," into a psychiatric hospital one Mother's Day. Through no choice of my own, the state mandated it due to events of the prior day. Let me explain…

At 4:30 p.m., the Knob Noster High School bus pulled up in front of our house. Kat did not get off. The absence of the beautiful, bright, and sometimes goofy girl that I'd see hop off the bus from my living room window (because meeting her outside would embarrass her) stung like a hornet. My normal routine was cruelly disrupted; my heart was immediately beating in overdrive. I knew something was not right. Call it a "mother's intuition." I went into problem-solving mode. (I'll dig deeper into this technique in a future chapter.) Admittedly, for a moment, I wanted to freak out. I was scared and concerned. But I knew I needed to remain calm, think clearly, and act quickly.

I first called Kat, but her cell phone went to voicemail. Next, I called the school and was connected to the superintendent, "Ms. Smith."

"I am looking for my daughter, Kat," I said in a calm voice. "She did not arrive home today."

"One second…" I heard the faint clicking of computer keys, and then Ms. Smith informed me, "It looks like she took the bus home."

"No, I am afraid she did not," I corrected her. "I just watched the bus leave. She did not get off it today."

"Have you checked with her friends?" Ms. Smith suggested.

"I'll do that next, but in the meantime, can you please check around the school for her?" I swallowed hard. "Something feels off."

"I'll investigate and call you back," she replied and disconnected.

I placed calls to some of her closest friends. No one had any idea where Kat was. The superintendent did a search of the school grounds, then went to my daughter's locker, where she found Kat's phone and a handwritten letter.

Ms. Smith paraphrased the letter to me. It was both a call for help and a decision to run away. It hinted at suicidal thoughts and concluded that she was going to follow the train tracks to find a dog at an animal shelter.

I called my husband, "Brett," a lieutenant colonel at Whiteman AFB, where we also lived, and informed him of the situation. He phoned the police and fire department, who stopped all rail systems coming in and out of our town.

Hours seemed like days, and the night turned frigid. The nearby town, Knob Noster, was very small, with a population of next to nothing. It had one stop sign and a couple of small businesses. My daughter was headed on foot to Warrensburg, the next town over, about five miles away. All I could think about was her being alone in the cold at night with the possibility of coyotes on the prowl. My heart ached for her safety.

My thoughts bounced back and forth between, *I am not a good mom* and *I wasn't there in time for my mom before her passing*. This knockout was hard to stomach. What did I miss? How did I miss it? This human, sent to me to protect and love, was wandering alone in the wild. How did I miss the pain that she so clearly felt, leading her to run away?

I scoured her room, looking for any clue that would provide an answer. I found nothing. I dropped to my knees and began to pray. The minutes seemed like hours. And with each passing hour, my heart ached more.

Six hours later, the phone rang. They found her! The Knob Noster Police Department discovered her taking refuge under a bridge a couple of miles outside town. She'd been frightened by some bats, prompting her to make a call from an old, discontinued iPhone she'd taken with her that still allowed emergency calls. She was safe and unharmed, from coyotes anyway.

I could breathe again. Brett and I drove to the station to bring her home. The look in her eyes was something I'll never forget. Although her innocence shone through the tears, the look on her face reminded me of the one I'd give my mother when I knew I'd done something wrong. I could not be upset with her. My heart was immeasurably grateful to see her alive and standing across from me. My arms wrapped around her, and tears fell down my face. I thanked God for returning her to me.

"I love you, Kat. I am so thankful you're safe," I cried out, squeezing her body into mine.

We sat in the police department filling out reports, and I couldn't help but notice her outfit. She was in leggings, multiple pairs of socks to her knees, and Converse tennis shoes. On her person were multiple sling bags, one filled with dog food for the pet she was determined to rescue. It turned out that the only rescuing that needed to be done that day was hers.

She had very little to say that night. Like most teenagers, she hid her pain and depression deep below the multiple layers of clothing she thought would keep her safe on her journey, seeking freedom from the battles she was fighting deep within her soul.

My baby was home, and I thought we'd be able to start some sort of healing process and discuss why she'd run away. But that could not have been further from what this world had in store for us. A couple of days later, the police department called to inform us that a judge had decided Kat needed to be admitted to the psychiatric institute in Warrensburg, ironically, the same city she'd attempted to run away to. The suicidal nature of her letter and a variety of other previous events I didn't know about led to this judge's decision "for her own safety." So, on that Mother's Day, against my will and hers, I walked my daughter into a psych ward.

This was my first time in a psychiatric institution. I'd seen them portrayed on TV shows and movies numerous times, but walking her down the hall to check her in gave me an indescribable feeling of dread. Deep down in my gut, I knew my daughter did not belong here. The energy was eerie... a building full of lost souls. A nurse placed an ID bracelet on her wrist. Her belongings were stripped from her person. I had no defense left. I clearly had "lost the round."

Brett and I were allowed a supervised visit once a week. Kat's progress seemed minimal, but this situation opened our eyes to a deeper issue she'd been fighting with internally. After multiple visits with Kat and her therapist, we found out that, besides fighting depression, she was engaging in self-harm through cutting, which had long been prevalent in her life.

We'd first discovered the self-harm when she was thirteen. At the time, we lived in Alaska, stationed at Joint Base Elmendorf-Richardson. When we had brought the behavior up to her counselor at school, the response was, "This is normal for teenagers. Watch it, but communication with a therapist is the best remedy." Kat had been seeing a therapist for some time, but peer pressure seemed to trump any sort of therapist's advice and treatment.

Then, when she ran away, it was yet another cry for help. She returned home a couple of months later from the psych ward unhealed, but her eyes were opened to what life would look like if something didn't change. Brett and I were also more aware that the situation required consistent attention.

The years that followed continued to be rough. The challenges and trials tested my faith and perseverance as a parent. I did my best to recall my youth, particularly my teenage years, yet it was still difficult to relate to the mind of my teenage daughter. I'd pray daily to take the pain, anxiety, and depression away from her. I'd beg for answers and solutions I could implement to help make Kat's life better. But the answers weren't coming fast enough.

It would not be until multiple years later that I'd begin to understand the meaning behind the incredible depth of pain and depression Kat struggled with.

Maybe you're standing in what feels like the biggest fight of your life or interceding and fighting for someone you love. And it feels exposed, like your battle is unfolding under bright lights with every moment seen and felt. Gasping for your final breath, in what could be your last round, you picked this book in hopes of finding a prescription to alleviate your pain. Your energy is depleted. Blood, sweat, and tears have significant meaning to you. You don't look like yourself or feel like yourself. Praying for reinforcements, this is not how you thought your life would play out.

Sucker punches, true to their name, come out of nowhere. Unexpected, in the gut, to the kidney, or straight to the jaw. Life will get its fair share of hits. Some, like the jab, are meant to distract you or get your attention. Others can come as a powerful "cross to the face," intended to knock you out if you're not prepared. Regardless of the size, getting hit does damage. It will make an impact on you and those around you based on your reaction or response to the hit. These hits and battles will make or break you.

Not only is it my intention to help you take hits with grace and gratitude, but also to equip you with the techniques to get right back up on your feet. You will take some hits, and inevitably, you may even be knocked out. This book is that lifeline to get you back in the ring, fighting back. Picture me in your corner, wrapping your hands, preparing you for the fight.

You may be gasping for air right now or feeling a bit delirious. Maybe you went down hard and don't even feel like you can get up, and reading this book is your last shout-out for help.

"For I know the plans I have for you," declares the Lord, "plans to prosper you and not to harm you, plans to give you hope and a future."

–Jeremiah 29:11

I get it. I feel your pain. I know how much it hurts. But pain is temporary. I promise you, there is a fighter within you. We just need to peel back the layers, rebuild, and ignite your inner champion. Suffering exposes us to our highest selves, builds character, and better prepares us for future battles. Getting knocked down is a given; getting up and moving forward is a choice. I encourage you, and I stand with you now, to make the choice. Choose you. Choose the destiny you're meant to fulfill.

Fight.

ROUND 1 TAKEAWAYS

1. There is an illuminating lesson to be learned within every battle.
2. As a fighter, it's not about *if* you will be called to fight, but *when.*
3. Suffering exposes a person to their highest self.
4. Your reason for fighting is so much bigger than you can imagine. Choose to fight.

Round 2

UNLEASH THE FIGHTER WITHIN

"The secret of change is to focus all your energy, not on fighting the old, but on building the new."
–Socrates

In this ring we call life, we'll face many opponents. We'll get knocked down, stepped on, and sucker punched, and we'll lose rounds. You'll also find that you'll come head-to-head with the same opponent or enemy more than once. This happens because we continue to repeat patterns that don't serve us if we failed to learn the lesson the first time and we're not aligned with our best self. Yes, you will continue to fight the same battle until you learn your lesson.

That bears repeating:

REMINDER: You WILL find yourself in the same battle until you learn your lesson.

The key to unlocking the lesson is understanding *why* we repeat patterns that don't serve us and *why* we make these choices. This will also reduce time when in battle, eliminate reoccurrences, and upgrade your fighter IQ.

The choices we make in life are conditioned by our philosophies and beliefs. These philosophies and beliefs shape our thoughts, which then lead us to the choices we make. Our behavior is a reaction to those choices. Over time, we build behavioral patterns and habits based on our philosophies.

Most of us operate in autopilot mode daily without even recognizing it. Don't get me wrong, operating on autopilot is helpful in some situations. Let me explain: autopilot is productive in the form of healthy habits that serve us. For example, going to the gym daily or selecting nutrient-dense foods. Even programmed triggering techniques that remind us to be present equate to quality use of autopilot.

Conversely, harmful autopilot habits that don't serve us include hitting the snooze button, reacting instead of responding, and searching for the "negative" in situations, as opposed to finding gratitude.

To become the ultimate fighter, the best version of yourself, you need to first examine and evaluate your philosophies and beliefs. During this process, you'll likely discover that you have adopted some philosophies and beliefs that don't serve the image of the fighter you're destined to be. It'll be necessary to retrain your brain and reprogram your thoughts to rebuild and unleash yourself from the philosophies and beliefs that are interfering with who you're created to be. This is the only way you'll be able to get on the path to your passion, purpose, and destiny.

Labels

The earliest memory I have of labels goes back to first grade and my teacher, Mrs. Bower. I liked her right away; she had a presence about her. She reminded me of my mom with her long, flowing curls and smile that lit up the room. Even at a young age, I enjoyed learning. In my room at home, I'd set up classrooms and teach my siblings. Teaching others and learning were a passion of mine. I thoroughly enjoyed Mrs. Bower's class; she made learning fun, and for the most part, I always looked forward to going to school.

Then it was conference time, which kids either dreaded or looked forward to. I could not wait for my mom to hear Mrs. Bower's approval of my progress in class. I sat nearby at my desk, tracing letters in the shaving cream meant to keep me distracted as they discussed my academic performance. I overheard Mrs. Bower tell Mom that I was "a good student, listened well, and was kind to others." Then she went on to say, "But don't expect much when it comes to scholastics. Melissa is an average student. She doesn't rank high in comparison to her peers."

Okay, so I was an "average" student. At the time, I didn't understand "average" as a negative connotation. It was a label bestowed upon me by a trusted source, a teacher I admired and looked up to.

I carried this label with me throughout my adolescent years. My mother reminded me of it often when I'd bring home a report card with below-average marks of C's and below. I'd be distraught and somewhat concerned because my peers were ecstatic about their straight A's and sometimes hinted that my parents would be disappointed in my performance.

My surprise would wear off year by year as Mom responded to my grades with, "It's okay, Lissa. That's good for an average student." I'd never get punished, reprimanded, or looked down upon for below-stellar marks.

I continued to live with this label, and it became me: "Average Melissa." I'd never see straight A's or a 4.0 GPA. The Dean's list, principal's list, honor roll, and advanced classes would never be in my future. I was placed in remedial English courses and had to retake algebra twice. However, my English teacher, Mrs. Marks, praised me often and encouraged me to "give it your best," because she believed in me. I could do that. My best was hard work. It was an immense feeling of pride when I finished at the top of remedial English, having the work done for the semester in a matter of weeks, and I could not understand why this class seemed so easy. (It was the teacher's praise and belief in me, I'd later come to learn.) Mrs. Marks gave me permission to be more than average. I continued to struggle in other classes but always had the excuse, "It's okay, I am *average*."

Jumping this "average" hurdle seemed far out of my reach. Although I wanted to excel, learning was becoming less fun for me. The lack of belief from most of my teachers and my mom that I could do better than average far outweighed the belief I had from that one teacher, Mrs. Marks, and the belief I had in myself. Once the truth of it sank in, I always felt out of place being average.

Have you ever put on an item of clothing and it just doesn't feel right? It itches, or the tag bugs you, or you have outgrown this article of clothing. Or the shoes pinch your toes. That became this "average" label. I was uncomfortable with this label; it never quite fit. I'd always admired the smart kids and deep down wanted to be part of that group. Throughout the years, I'd contemplate, "Why not me?"

It wasn't until my junior year in high school that I'd come across another teacher who'd see a light in me. It'd been dimmed down so far that I couldn't turn it back on all by myself. Mr. Hyams, my U.S. History teacher, brought history to life! He sparked a flame in me that opened my eyes to possibility again. I'd wake up excited to go to school and attend his class. His kind words, engagement with students, and belief in me started me on a path to "beyond average" that I am grateful for to this day. Assignment after assignment, test after test, lecture by lecture, my grades started to rise in his class. I completed Mr. Hyams' history class with a solid A. My first-ever A! Ecstatic and eager to learn more, I anxiously wanted to be part of his AP-level senior government class, called "We the People." This class required a teacher recommendation and enrollment in an advanced English class.

In the back of my mind, I replayed Mrs. Bower's, my mother's, and other teachers' "average" remarks. I recalled all the struggles I went through just to attain "C" marks throughout school. I doubted my ability to take an advanced English class, even though just a few years earlier, I had been placed in remedial English. Hesitation and insecurity ran deep through my mind, body, and soul as I dreamed of this lingering possibility to be more than "average."

But there was something in me, a "gut feeling," that told me I needed to push forward. To leave my comfort zone and give myself a shot. Mr. Hyams believed in me and gave a glowing recommendation for the government course, and he did the same with the English teacher. If he could believe in me, so could I. So I registered for both classes.

I entered my senior year of high school with newfound confidence. I'd spent all summer completing the homework required for the courses. Day after day, on dial-up Internet, I'd research and type up every lesson. I may not have been the smartest, but I knew that I could put in the time and outwork anyone. I was ready.

I still vividly remember my first day of senior year. I glowed from the inside out from feeling good about myself. I excelled all that year. I not only worked part-time in the fast-food industry and helped care for my siblings, but I also conquered two AP courses!

In my senior year, I graduated with a 3.86 GPA. It wasn't a 4.0, but so damn close! My hard work built competence, which led to greater confidence in myself. The work instilled the worth. With a great support system of my amazing teachers, that "average" label was dangling by a thread.

Unfortunately, the person who should have been my biggest supporter and should have been in my corner from the start was my mom. She saw my newfound belief in myself as a mistake. I don't fault her for not believing in me, because I understand better now that I am older and have new knowledge. I wasn't aware of it then, but as I started to rip this "average" label off and excel, Mom thought I was going crazy. My above-average marks and confidence in myself initiated a referral to my counselor and to a therapist, because Mom thought there was something mentally wrong with me. She thought I was acting so outside my "average" label and our family cycle that this caused a huge separation between us.

At the time, I found it difficult to understand why Mom would have me sent to therapy for performing at an above-average level. Today, though, I can acknowledge that Mom was only reacting according to her own limiting beliefs.

* * *

What has been stopping you? Plain and simple, *you*! The only thing that has kept you from becoming the champion you're destined to be is the label you're continuing to operate and live in. What label are you living with right now? Who are you allowing to write your story? Is this label serving you or interfering with your destiny?

At times, unknowingly, we live our lives as a product of our environment. The people you're surrounded by, the neighborhoods you grew up in, the schools you've attended, the relationships you've been involved in. All these experiences and situations have sculpted you and attached a label to you, and you've accepted it.

"Average" is the label that I lived with for over a decade. My entire childhood was molded around it until I decided to make a change. As children, we can be brainwashed into this belief of what our life should entail. As we enter adulthood and can think on our own, it becomes our responsibility to change the cycle. It's hard. It requires work and reprogramming your philosophies so you don't continue the same patterns. The good news is: *you* can decide to make a change.

Certain labels strip you of your true identity and, consequently, of your potential. Underneath a label, there's a fighter waiting to emerge. This label will be your biggest enemy. It'll continue to battle your body, mind, and spirit. Trapped deep in your subconscious, these beliefs rule over you and will continue to write your story until you take the pen back.

It's time to rip off the label that no longer serves you and replace it with the words fighters and champions go to battle with.

REMINDER: You don't have to be a product of your environment.

As I said earlier, I signed up to join the military when I was a junior in high school. I needed a plan going into my senior year that assured me I wouldn't continue my family's cycle of poverty and scarcity mindset. I needed a way to pay for college. Nobody in my family had gone to college. A degree represented a way out, a way to blast myself out of this cycle of generational poverty.

Mom raised all four of us alone while she managed a full-time job. She did not go to college; she married young and fell victim to ongoing unfavorable relationships. Mom was quite capable of making sure we had what we needed to get by. We always had food on the table, whether it came from food stamps, the local food pantry, or the church. Mom made it a game, and we never knew what poverty really was. I recall learning to count out food items with food stamps we had available or dashing through the grocery store, racing my sibling to find the next item on the WIC check. I never fully understood why we had to have our house inspected and approved by a government agency called "Section 8 Housing." However, I do recall that Mom would pass with flying colors every time, because her standards for herself were the highest, and she always wanted to present her best.

Mom worked hard away from home. This necessitated that I take an early parental role with my siblings. I learned quickly how to take care of others. I never saw this as abnormal. This was our life. I enjoyed helping my mom; we were a team, and her approval meant the world to me.

My mom worked so hard; she quickly adapted to whatever position or job she was placed in. Climbing her way to the top and serving others came very naturally to her. No matter the job, Mom always showed up and gave her best. No task was beneath her. There was nothing she could not learn to do. Mom had the initiative and drive to make the most of wherever she had been placed.

I could never make sense, even with my stellar math skills, of how she could make so little money go so far. I'd see her paychecks and could not understand how she was able to support all of us. But she did. My mother operated as a fighter. Later on, I did realize that, despite her ability to provide, we were struggling, and I wanted to help in any way possible.

Joining the military provided a way for me to pay for college. I knew my grades would never get me a scholarship. And there definitely was not going to be any financial help available from Mom. The military was a no-brainer for me. I could learn valuable skills, gain experience, have a roof over my head, and have food in my belly.

My Air Force recruiter resembled Nicholas Cage. He spoke of "possibility" if I listened, showed up, and worked hard. I understand now that this may have just been a great sales pitch, but for an average student with no money, this resonated deeply with me. I had hope that I'd found a way to help provide some extra money for Mom. However, leaving my family concerned me.

I started working part-time at age fourteen. I was allowed twenty work hours a week while I went to school. I started in fast food, and my paychecks went directly to support my family. They were small, but everything helped. I was always grateful that I could help out and was nervous that even without this small amount, if I were to leave, it would be detrimental to my family. Also, who would help my siblings?

If I had listened to my environment and the people around me, I would've continued to live an average life. I'd be financially poor. I received a lot of ridicule for fighting the norm that my family had created and going against the grain. College potential and military service? The only other family member to join the military was my grandfather during World War II. He fought against the Germans and became a POW. I had a burning desire for more. I knew I was capable of more. Deep down, I knew I needed to resist what had become the norm for my family.

It was a lot scarier to remain in my current situation than to experience the unknown and risk possible failure. I knew I had to make a move. That's why I enlisted. It was not about me; it was about changing my family life cycle.

* * *

What label (or labels) do you continue to live with from your childhood or past? Did you grow up financially poor? Do you have a family line of health issues and believe it's in your genetics to be overweight, depressed, or have anxiety? Did you watch your parents struggle in relationships, so you figured, *why wouldn't I?*

Some labels are caught, not taught. My mother did not teach me to have a poor mindset; I caught on to the lifestyle. There are so many labels we'll attach to ourselves that affect our decisions daily and impact our thoughts and behaviors.

It's time to start questioning your beliefs. You can choose what part of your past you will continue to carry with you. You can extract lessons from your history and use them as guides. Dig through that mess. Wipe away the pain and reveal lessons that will serve you. I know this is tough and uncomfortable. It's time to change your belief about discomfort. We grow from discomfort when we *choose* to. Turn your burden into a blessing. You'll come out of this battle a stronger, more vibrant fighter if you choose to do the work. If you choose the temporary discomfort.

We get to decide what our story looks like. When you take back the pen and redefine your past experiences to serve you, your world starts to resemble possibility. Hope returns. You will step back onto the battlefield as a warrior.

Look around. We're a byproduct of the environment we allow ourselves to consume. What are you listening to? What words do you speak? What are you watching, whether it's on TV or social media? ALL OF IT matters. The good old saying holds true: "Garbage in, garbage out."

You must be willing to ask yourself, *Is my environment serving my destiny? Am I stepping into the right rings? Is the battlefield I am on even a battle I should be in?*

REMINDER: Change the way you think about yourself, and you can change your life. What you're not changing, you're choosing.

Not allowing my past to define me but sculpting myself into the fighter I am today has been one of the most difficult, uncomfortable, and challenging processes I have ever gone through. Most times (okay, a lot of the time), I would cry in disbelief and confusion. I'd question the universe and God, as my spirituality and relationship with God were minimal at this point in my life: *What is the meaning behind this situation? Why me?*

* * *

For much of my adulthood, it was difficult for me to admit that I struggled with self-acceptance and lacked self-approval in my physical appearance. I think most women go through this phase at some point in their lives. We're our toughest critics, right? But for me, it went so much deeper than that. Layer upon layer of low self-esteem needed to be peeled back.

My acceptance of myself started back in high school. I was often made fun of for being too skinny. To top that off, I had a massive overbite. Combine that with being a below-average student, and I didn't have much to fall back on.

The military made sense to me, and not just from a financial standpoint. It also provided an opportunity to prove my worth. I married young at age nineteen, about a year after joining the Air Force. Call me a hopeless romantic, but I'd convinced myself that marriage would demonstrate my value. I was eager to prove to everyone back home that I was good enough to be wanted by someone. Unfortunately, when you get married while not knowing who you are and not truly understanding your worth, you will also accept someone who is not worthy of you. You will be undervalued and mistreated.

When you don't value yourself, you cannot expect others to see your value either. Three failed marriages and three kids later, I finally learned this lesson. (More to follow on this soon.)

Your belief in yourself needs to be solid before jumping into a relationship. Don't expect from others what you cannot provide yourself. Although in shock, ashamed, and discouraged, I had three amazing angels to remind me why every heartbreak brings with it a lesson of joy.

REMINDER: Turn those burdens into blessings!

At the beginning of this chapter, I talked about how we'll often find ourselves facing the same opponents and fighting the same battles. When your beliefs and philosophies change, so do your thoughts, behaviors, and actions. You start to attract quality people and ideal situations into your world. If you don't change your beliefs, whether it's in yourself or about your lifestyle, you will continue to face the same struggles until you learn the lesson. The definition of insanity is doing the same thing over and over and expecting a different result. You must do the hard work and make a significant change.

Been There, Done That

I can speak firsthand about jumping into failed relationships and marriages. In 2013, I was a single mom working a full-time job and attending school full-time, and I had started my first business in the fitness industry as a personal trainer. I stepped onto the battlefield every day, fighting for myself and my children.

And then it happened again. I met someone. This was not my first rodeo. I should've known better. I should've done the work. Plain and simple, I thought I had. I'd spent about a year working on myself. I was doing all the right things. Then a "knight in shining armor" rode up on his horse, ready to save my children and me. He promised to put me in a castle where we'd live "happily ever after." I was excited for my new role as the wife of a military commander; in fact, I had the opportunity to attend a one-week course on how to act accordingly, which also turned into our honeymoon. My husband invited me to quit my job, business, and school and move across the country with my two children to start a new life. I was excited and anxious all at the same time.

Strangely, warning signals went off in my head: *Alert! Alert! You barely know this guy. And now you're going to jump into a car with him and drive off to start a new life?*

Of course, I did! It was a dream come true for me. This man promised me the world and said the most important words to me: "I love you." So, we did it. A proposal, a promotion (for him), and a PCS (Permanent Change of Station, for those unfamiliar with military lingo). "The three Ps!" he joked in his farewell speech. His new "family in a box" was good to go!

We moved to another state where I knew nobody. My fairytale quickly turned into a horror story. I had no job or friends, and I relied solely on him. I was to play the part of his wife in his military world while simultaneously being a mother. I knew this when I signed my name on the marriage license. I was no stranger to the military and most of its expectations. I was ready and eager to serve him and his squadron (those he led). And I did just that. I'd show up not just as his stay-at-home wife and a mother, but as his spouse, his partner in command, selflessly serving in all roles. I never expected anything in return, and I thoroughly enjoyed serving in all capacities. I find joy in serving.

But what was difficult for me to understand was his consistent disregard for me as a wife and a partner. From the beginning, he was never there for me. The way he ignored and dismissed me, I felt like I was just another piece of furniture in his house. He'd make excuses about his energy being depleted. Other excuses for his ice-cold distance ran rampant. At first, I believed him. I figured the neglect and lack of partnership must be all my fault, and therefore, I should be able to fix it. Doing my best to appease him, just like in past relationships, I fell back to negative patterns of "people pleasing" instead of setting boundaries. I tried for five years to fix myself. To fix the constant neglect I was getting. I felt so alone and unwanted, even though there was another human, my husband, right there.

There were times when the comfort of my pillow and the security of my blanket wrapped around my frail body would win against the challenges I thought the day would bring. It was easier to stay tucked in tight and give up on my dreams than it was to get uncomfortable and fight whatever monsters lurked outside the fort I had created to protect me.

I'd lie awake at night worrying, overthinking, and then cry myself to sleep. Some nights I couldn't sleep at all. This nightmare I was in ate away at my dreams every day. I wasn't even in the ring anymore. I had no fight left; I tapped out. I watched the titles I had fought for so desperately just months prior to the big move slip from my grip: business owner, independent woman, unconditionally loved child of God, honor roll student, happy mother, self-sufficient, one by one… gone.

I came to the point of raising the white flag. I needed to surrender. I did not recognize who I was anymore. It was difficult to function day in and day out. I'd put on a fake smile to conceal my insecurities and pain. Most days, I wanted to give up and say, "Fuck it all!"

I had been here before. This place was all too familiar. It was another low for me. Think: bottom feeder. Yes, *me*, the girl who looked like she had her shit together on the outside, had arrived back at destination "self-pity"… again. I'd started multiple businesses. I have multiple degrees. People would come to me for advice and answers. Yet again, I found myself trapped in this foxhole, taking hits from the enemy with no reprieve in sight.

Have you ever experienced a nightmare where you so badly wanted it to end? It felt so real that you'd wake up sweating or in tears. The vivid images would replay in your head, reminding you of the trauma you experienced that night. That is exactly what I was experiencing. I was screaming for help, desperately waiting for someone to come and save me, or at least send backup. Reinforcements were nowhere to be found. My nightmare was my reality, and the only ally I had was myself. Unfortunately, at the time, I was useless to myself and to everyone else.

Can I get a show of hands if you have been in a similar situation? I know it's hard to admit sometimes, because admitting it makes it a reality and a truth you must face. You're tucked into your bed so tight that the thought of getting out seems impossible. It's difficult to admit, but you're no longer living; you're experiencing a slow death. You watch yourself being buried alive. The dirt is being dropped onto your coffin. Your head is resting comfortably on a pillow. The fighter buried deep inside desperately wants to resurface, but how?

You may feel alone, isolated, empty, discouraged, and afraid. But one thing I can promise you is you're not alone. Many have crawled through these same battlefields and triumphed. It's your time. It's GO time. Decide to make a change. Declare, "Enough is enough!" It's time to not just pull back the blankets that secure you in this isolation; it's time to rip them off and proclaim you will fight again! Choose to get up. Stand up tall. Announce out loud, "I still have fight left!"

Seriously, I want you to find a bed and jump on it like you're a kid again! Repeat to yourself: *I still have fight left! I am a fighter! I have purpose!* You may not feel it yet, but after each repetition, your fighter will begin to emerge.

Do you remember playing dress-up as a child? Putting on a costume or a wig, grabbing a doll, or a sword? We could decide to be whoever we wanted to be. We could go wherever our imagination would take us. Our dreams were big and unconditional.

As adults, we play similar games. We wear these masks of who we think we should be. Of what society expects us to be. And we cover up the pain, discomfort, and ugliness to preserve ourselves and function in our daily lives. We play a role; we merely act on stage, dressed in the comfort of our denial. Life is conditional under these terms.

What innately happens during this process is that we barely get by. Functioning in everyday life becomes difficult. We live in a conditional environment, just barely staying comfortable. We compromise our values, goals, and purpose because we're afraid.

Change will disrupt our norms, but it requires hard work. It forces us to step outside our comfort zone. The fear stems from myriad thoughts:

upsetting or disappointing friends, family, lovers, coworkers; doing something we have never done before; fear of success or growth; and unworthiness. Imposter syndrome runs deep within us.

What happens if we don't change is that we end up merely existing in our own lives. Someone *else* is writing your story. Conditions dictate your next chapter. You end up just doing your best to survive. We miss important moments with our children, friends, and family. We become complacent, and mediocrity becomes our norm. Without even realizing it, every day we lose a piece of the incredible potential of the fighter we were destined to become. Before you know it, you don't even recognize yourself anymore. Deep down, an even greater pain starts to boil. It's haunting; it pulls at your soul. You feel incomplete.

You will always have that yearning to become more because a fighter never loses their purpose. There's no escaping it. You have been chosen. However, it's up to you to fight. Nobody can do that for you. So, what's stopping you?

REMINDER: Fear is only as deep as the mind allows.

I'll be the first to admit that I can be hardheaded. Learning to let go, learning to listen, and giving up control all did not come easily to me. I struggled, and I still do. We all will. No one is perfect, and, well, that is what fighters understand. I didn't know my worth or comprehend who I was. It took time and many battles to clear out the damage that had been done in my past.

After multiple failed relationships, I continued to put myself in yet another relationship with a man who was not right for me. Did you notice

I said that I continued to place *myself* in these unhealthy, unworthy relationships? I attracted men into my world who filled holes. I was damaged and broken; thus, I attracted damaged and broken. I saw myself as an object and unworthy. So, I attracted others into my world who'd use me to satisfy *their* wants and needs. I was looking for approval and love from people through an outlet that couldn't be filled, yet I pushed and ached for it. Usually ending in emotional and physical trauma, relationship after relationship, the hits were taken one after the next.

My image of my body and beauty held no value. My self-worth was tainted. I did not feel whole. The pain ran deep. I did not recognize my own reflection because I was so desperate for acceptance and approval from others. I'd given myself so many labels that did not serve my inner fighter; at this point, a fighter in me couldn't even be recognized. I'd been used and abused like property. I'd trapped myself in a hole of hopelessness. My heart ached for change. My soul wanted to grasp onto some sort of understanding. But, thankfully, in my pit of self-sorrow, a still, small voice could be heard, and it whispered, "You're a fighter."

Your Given Label

In my late thirties, I'd forgotten who I was, and honestly, I never really understood the magnitude of what I am. As I lay there listening to this still small voice, my heart began to fill with a sense of healing and relief that I'll never forget. It was like a rope had been tossed down into the dark hole where my body lay. The voice spoke softly to me: "You're the daughter of a King." I was reminded that I was not alone. Getting knocked so far down left me only one option: to look up and listen. Never again would I allow myself to surrender to the enemy.

This enemy was no stranger. In fact, this enemy of defeat, self-doubt, fear, and unworthiness would rear its mean little head anytime I'd get close to a breakthrough, but not any longer. This was the last time I'd allow life to just happen to me. I was no longer a victim. I am worthy, I am unconditionally loved, and I don't need another person to validate that.

"If you can look up, you can get up."
–Les Brown

I grew up in the LDS, or Mormon, religion for nearly all of my childhood. I was required, like most kids, to attend church with my mother and siblings. And yet, I never had a relationship with my Savior. In fact, I often questioned the religion as I progressed through school and never took it too seriously.

The small voice that whispered could not be ignored. I felt a strength beyond myself. I felt comforted. A song that we sang in church played in my head: "I am a Child of God." I began to weep and raised my hands into the air. "Please, Lord, lead me, guide me, walk beside me, and help me find the way."

It was up until this point that I had allowed relationships, people, and my environment to define and label me. I had allowed the world to clutter my mind, body, and soul. Not any longer. I decided then and there to take back my power, reclaim my greatness, and surrender the labels that did not serve me.

I am the child of the Most High God. I am the daughter of a King. I am enough, regardless of my relationship status, job, or mistakes. I am perfect and made in His image.

"If God is for us, who can be against us?"
–Romans 8:31, NKJV

We're all children of God, the Most High King. The label that defines all labels. Have you forgotten that, like I did? Or maybe you have never been made aware of your royalty? The chaos of the world, our environment, and the people we surround ourselves with can quickly tarnish our given value if we consent to it.

Realizing and understanding this, my world began to evolve in ways I could not imagine. As I continued to listen to the still, small voice and understand my worth, my testimony grew with every "coincidence" that occurred.

REMINDER: Faith untested can not be trusted.

This transformation didn't happen, though, until I accepted the empowering label "I am a child of God." Part of accepting is believing it. I had to reprogram my brain to understand this first; then my thoughts and actions would follow appropriately. I had to unbecome everything that I had become, to be what I was created to be: a child of God. I eliminated excuses with my newfound belief and turned them into reasons to get up, "wrap up," and fight for myself and my kids each day.

* * *

Have you forgotten who you really are? Have you allowed a label to define you and determine your worth? What label (or labels) are you living with that needs to be removed so you can stop fighting the same losing battles repeatedly? What defeating philosophies do you hold that create the patterns of behavior that don't serve you? When was the last time you inventoried your environment?

It's time for a pattern interrupt. Eliminate the labels that no longer promote you as a warrior. What we're not actively changing, we're choosing. It's time to get to work. It's time to start unleashing the fighter within.

ROUND 2 TAKEAWAYS

1. Your given label is the ONLY label that defines you. You're a child of the Most High God who loves you more than anyone on earth will ever love you. Focus on that love and that partnership.

2. Inventory and audit your beliefs and labels. What needs to be updated, removed, or added?

3. Change the way you think about yourself, and you can change your life.

4. What you're not changing, you're choosing.

Round 3

GET IN THE RING OF LIFE

"Crave the result so intensely that the work is irrelevant."
–Tim Grover

From what I have written so far, some might conclude that I am a hot mess. That is a fact. Most of my day, I operate at the level of "hot mess" unless, you guessed it, I am sleeping. If you were to ask me how my day is going, my usual response is, "Wonderfully chaotic." This is not by accident. Perspective is everything. How you choose to see your day and what you choose to participate in are up to you. There is a difference between letting life happen to you versus you happening to your life. Once I accepted that I get to choose how I see my world, it became simple.

My day is very intentional, structured, and full of surprises (thank God). As an entrepreneur, mother, and athlete, I have come to accept that my day will be full of wonderful chaos. I choose to operate and live at this level of "comfortable with discomfort."

One of the biggest lessons I've learned as a fighter is this: if you're not moving, you're not progressing. If you're not failing, you're not trying hard enough or taking enough chances. If you're not moving, progressing, failing, and learning, chances are you're not truly living and not succeeding, which in happenstance usually means you're, well, dying a very slow death. We die at 75, but some of us stopped living at 25.

As a fighter, it's not in my DNA to sit still and let life happen to me. If you have identified as a fighter (chances are likely because you're still reading), it's not in your DNA to become complacent either. You crave change, results, and progress. You have a *strong* desire to contribute to society. Mediocrity and the status quo frustrate you. There is a burning desire in your soul to, as David Meltzer, my mentor and dear friend, points out, "Consistently, persistently, without quitting, pursue your potential every day."

As fighters, we're destined to be in the ring of life. On the field of battle is where we find peace and satisfaction. It's a requirement that every day we "wrap up" and embrace the discomfort of forward progress. This requires discipline, determination, hard work, and sacrifice. Once I understood this concept, accepting my responsibilities and position as a warrior was simple. Now, I said simple, not easy. Once you understand and accept your destiny as a fighter, it's time to prepare yourself for the challenges, tests, and trials that loom ahead.

As I have shared in previous chapters, I've been a warrior in many battles, facing my fair share of trials and tribulations. Honestly, I feel like God placed his hand on the top of my fragile little head and said, "My dear, you will face a multitude of challenges, and they will sculpt and mold you into the champion fighter I know you are." There is a reason behind the season you're in.

Let me repeat that: **There is a reason behind the season you're in.**

As a fighter, you need to be prepared at all times, hands wrapped, gloves on, and ready to respond to these challenges, storms, and sucker punches that come your way. How you respond to these trials will determine your next chapter, your next move, potential downtime, and whether or not you fulfill your destiny. Perspective is important, but being as prepared as possible is equally necessary.

It's inevitable that when we decide to fulfill our destiny, the universe is going to test us to make sure we really want it. That's what these battles are all about. How you decide to respond in these battles is what matters. You get to decide now, knowing that you will be in battle, if you're going to show up as a victim or a fighter. Because you're reading this book again, I'm going to presume we'll be wrapping up your hands, lacing up your gloves, and entering the ring.

As C.S. Lewis points out, "Hardships often prepare ordinary people for an extraordinary destiny."

I am nothing special, as I have established in previous chapters. I am normal and very much human. We're all very similar; the difference is the choices we make. These decisions will either take us one step closer to our destiny or, in some cases, two steps back.

The word "decide" is powerful. It means to come to a resolution, to rule out other options. You see, even when you think you're not deciding to choose your destiny to propel yourself forward, you're still making a choice to not fulfill your potential. To opt not to decide is also a decision. There are always options.

To simplify it for you, I'll give you a tool I use quite often when deciding about a situation, circumstance, or challenge. I ask myself this question: "Does this decision put me one step closer to my destiny?"

Replace "decision" with "relationship," "choice," "habit," "event," or whatever situation you may be facing. If the decision is not aligned with your purpose, it's an easy no. Likewise, when you're in the middle of a painful battle and you know it aligns with your purpose, you can breathe easier knowing that every struggle you're facing is priming you. That every hit you're taking is positioning you one step closer to your ultimate destiny. When you decide to take back the pen and control the narrative of your story, backed by purpose and positioning you toward your destiny, you enter the ring as a fighter and not a victim.

The fight may still feel daunting at times. The hits you take can become intolerable. It can still feel like giant, insurmountable challenges surround you. I did say it would not be easy. When you stand firm on a foundation that is built on strong beliefs, truths, promises, and most importantly, God, you enter the battlefield with strength and confidence. Your confidence will continue to increase with every battle because you build competence through doing the work. And before you know it, your faith has increased, and you enter your next battle stronger and with even more belief in yourself and your ally, God. But you must get in the fight. Choose to fight.

It's GO time, fighter.

REMINDER: If God puts a Goliath in front of you, he must believe there is a David inside of you.

You must embrace the struggle, knowing that the reason behind the battle is so much bigger than you can imagine or understand at this current moment. Know that what you're experiencing right now in this season, in this chapter of your life, is just that. It's a moment. It's a round. It's but a chapter, or even just a page, in your story.

I want to reinforce this point, because not every time you get in the ring will you feel like you have won that round. Not every battle will seem like a victory bell ringing in your favor. Not all seasons will be warm, sunny, and comfortable. However, here is the ringer: What you extract from these challenges will determine what your *next* chapter looks like. How you respond versus react will influence recovery time. Choosing to look at each loss as a lesson and an opportunity to grow will elevate you. Every decision we make has consequences. Every choice we make dictates how much closer we move toward our destiny. Every challenge is a door opening to an opportunity. Will you step through it?

I know it's difficult to face each battle head-on with optimism and positivity. I am not demanding that you do so every single time. In fact, sometimes your first instinct will be not to respond; you may have an emotional reaction. Depending on the opponent you're facing at the time, the magnitude of the punch coming at you may shock you, and you could get hit in the face with disbelief and possibly "black out" for a few moments. What I want you to remember is this: The battle you're facing does not change your DNA. It does not alter your fighter status. It does not change what you can accomplish and overcome.

There will be chapters and pages in your story that downright suck. But remember who you are and what you are. Everything you need to triumph is already within you. God does not call the qualified; he qualifies the called. And you, my friend, are called to be a fighter.

Embrace The Suck

I have mentioned quite a few times that charging toward our destiny, maximizing our potential, and operating as a fighter won't be easy. But it can become "easier" if you decide now to *embrace the suck.*

I am writing this segment of my book as America (and the world) is experiencing the impact of the rampant COVID-19 pandemic. "Coronavirus" is now a word in my five-year-old daughter's vocabulary. COVID-19 is now a defining era in our history. A pandemic that has forever altered our everyday norms. I write this from the viewpoint of a business owner, entrepreneur, and mother.

March 17, 2020, is a day I'll never forget. For me, it was a situation similar to September 11, 2001, when the NYC World Trade Center towers were hit. I was an airman at the time, in the USAF, about three months into my term of service. My fellow cadets and I stared at the TV screen in stunned silence as the news replayed over and over the South Tower and then the North Tower collapsing into dust and rubble. While still in disbelief, I was commanded to take emergency action as we prepared our fighter jets for takeoff. The entire country was in shock and awe. We had taken a major sucker punch right to the gut, and the battle that would forever alter the USA had started. We went to war against terrorism.

Almost twenty years later, during the COVID-19 pandemic, I had a similar shock-and-awe reaction when Colorado Governor Jared Polis announced the complete closure of in-person businesses on March 17, 2020. Before this announcement, attendance had already started to decrease in my three boutique gyms in Colorado Springs, as well as in restaurants and other public establishments across the United States. The virus had already stricken so many people, altering the normal way of life across the globe, and it continued to mercilessly advance across U.S. soil.

State after state was announcing business closures. And when it happened to me, my heart sank. I gasped for air, and it felt like my brain had turned off. I was hit with a sucker punch. Again.

Yes, I'd been sucker-punched before, and I'll never forget 9/11. But in those military situations, I had leader after leader directing my next move. I was a pawn on a chessboard following their commands. This time, however, COVID-19 was a situation that not only the USA wasn't prepared for, but most of the world wasn't either, including me.

I was in the driver's seat now. The survival of the gyms I'd built over the last two years depended on the decisions I'd make over the next couple of months. The choices I'd make would not only impact me but also my family, my team, and the members I'd become accustomed to serving every day. And it all fell on my shoulders. It was the heaviest weight I'd ever had to bear up until that point in my life. It was do-or-die time.

* * *

Two years ago was the anniversary of one of the biggest decisions I have ever made. First, I completed the required interview to see if I qualified to purchase the three 9Round locations. After I was deemed "good to go," I completed the required corporate training to obtain approval to join the 9Round team as an owner.

You heard me right; I decided it was in God's plan for me to purchase not one, but three gyms. The gyms weren't doing very well at the time. Thousands of dollars in updates were needed to bring them up to corporate standards. I'd started working as a trainer for one of the gyms and was quickly promoted to manager. Then, after that, I was on track to purchase three of them within three months. Serving as a Champion Trainer and owner at these gyms was a no-brainer for me. The business model just made sense. I'd never seen anything like it. I'd worked in the fitness industry and had started and stopped (thanks to the military) multiple fitness businesses around this time. From franchises to big box gyms, outdoor boot camps to personal training, I'd done it all up until this point. However, walking into 9Round Kickboxing Fitness, a concept that integrated kickboxing-themed workouts in a circuit training format with no class times, made too much sense not to say yes to an opportunity that was right up my alley. I knew I could not pass it up.

I had just returned from the 9Round headquarters. After meeting with the founder and franchisor, Shannon "the Cannon" Hudson, I was excited to come on board the 9Round train. However, after looking at the three franchise agreements that would lock me in for a minimum of ten years, honestly, it scared me a bit. That was a big commitment. I wouldn't be risking just my time and money but also time with my kids and my family's savings. It was a big deal to me. But it had also been a longtime dream of mine.

Doubt, fear, shock, excitement, and anxiety are just a few of the emotions I was feeling. Was I making the right decision? I had started various businesses before, but nothing on this scale.

"If you're passionate about the product, Melissa, and your mission, then go for it," Larry Leith, founder of the Tokyo Joes Asian food restaurant chain, advised me. When I walked into 9Round for my introductory workout, the feeling was overwhelming. Life-changing. I knew this was where I belonged. I fell in love at first workout. There was no question that I believed in the product. I had no doubt that this would be the vehicle that'd help me achieve my mission in life. I've said it before, but it bears repeating: When you make decisions with your purpose in mind, choices become clear. On top of that, the choices become simple to make.

My mission at that time was to transform lives through health and fitness. I felt like it was ethically my responsibility to educate as many people as possible about getting healthy before it's too late. This mission was born from the loss of my mother and the feeling of not being able to help her before it was too late.

What a difference two years makes. I was finally at a point in my businesses on March 17, 2020, where I had established a killer team of champion trainers that felt like family. We'd finally finished the required renovation and upgrades of the three gyms. And we'd just hit a point in the books where we were becoming profitable. The journey up to that point had been so demanding on time management, personal growth, and leadership.

Equally, it was just as rewarding. All the hard work I'd put in over the previous two years was starting to pay off in terms of profitability, peace of mind, and time freedom. We were living our mission to change lives, thirty minutes at a time. Our vision to help thousands fight the battle against obesity was unfolding in front of my eyes. My heart was so full, and I knew Mom would've been so proud of me.

The COVID-19 order to close down happened so quickly. Just like that: "Shut your doors to the public!" *What? This can't be happening to me! All that work. My team. Our members. My family. What am I going to do?* I felt like I was letting everyone down. I thought about the people who were placed in my path that I was given the responsibility to protect, guide, teach, and provide for. I stood there feeling so alone and confused.

The previous two years played through my mind like a movie. All the way back to the day I signed on the dotted line to take responsibility for these gyms and what they stood for. It was eerie how similar the feelings were. This was a test. How I would respond over the next few hours would determine the fate of this legacy I was building. And that's exactly what it was. The day of March 17, 2020, was an opportunity being presented to me, and it was my responsibility to accept the challenge to level up.

When you make choices with your purpose in mind, decisions become clear. I quickly decided to pivot within hours of the mandated close and transition all 600 members to online training. My mission and vision remained the same despite the governor's mandated shutdown. The only change was the vehicle for how I'd provide it. I had new challenges that required me to find new solutions.

You read the above correctly. In just hours, three to be exact, I transitioned to online training. Success loves speed. It was a no-brainer. My journey in life had prepared me for this exact moment. I immediately implemented systems to provide fun and effective programs for communication, accountability, and community, which was exactly what my members needed during this disruption they were facing in their lives as well.

During ten years of moving with husbands to five military bases and each time having to shut down multiple health and fitness endeavors, I'd investigated online training to provide to my clients when I was taken away physically due to these military-required moves. It was difficult to build one-on-one relationships and see clients progress, only to leave them, so I had to come up with a solution. I hired a coach and spent the better part of a year learning the ins and outs of how to run an online business. I made mistakes but remedied them much quicker and succeeded faster because the coach I hired had been there and done that.

My good fortune was that this training back in 2018 prepared me for the pandemic in 2020. Without it, I wouldn't have been able to pivot so quickly and ultimately save my businesses from permanent closure, as was the fate of so many other indoor gyms and fitness businesses. This online training prepared me to succeed. I already had everything inside of me that I needed to succeed.

REMINDER: Everything you need to succeed is already within you.

When was the last time you were in a similar situation? Not sure what to do, you felt alone, scared, and unsure of the next steps you should take.

It may not make sense at the time, but in hindsight, when we start to connect the dots, we see that our journey has a purpose. Learn to reframe the situations you're presented with. Look at challenges as opportunities to learn, grow, and level up. It's up to you to decide on how you're going to respond to these battles.

Had I not chosen to take defensive action, even in fear, the impact of COVID-19 could have permanently destroyed my business. Now, I'm not saying it was easy. I had to take over 95 percent of the responsibilities of my team. Additionally, while everyone seemed to have extra time on their hands to "Netflix and chill," I was working 12-plus-hour days to keep my business from disappearing. I had to embrace the suck. I was called to war, and I decided to fight.

When these battles occur, when you're called to war, what will you choose to do? Will you wrap up and fight? Or will you run the other way in fear of the unknown? Will you face these battles, knowing that you were called to fight and everything you need to win is already within you? Are you willing to embrace the pain and discomfort that comes with being a fighter?

Fighters become champions because they know that they must put in the work. Luck favors hard work. Fighters learn to embrace the suck and even enjoy it. Everything a fighter goes through prepares them for their next battle. Enjoy the season you're in, and understand that adversity is needed for optimal human development. If you have passion behind your purpose and work ethic, the adversities you face become exciting and exhilarating. Because deep down, you know without question that this fight is just a small part of your story. Added up, all these battles you'll come across are leading you to your next big win and to bring glory to all those you impact. It's time to fight, Champion.

ROUND 3 TAKEAWAYS

1. If you're not moving, you're not progressing.
2. Ask yourself: *Does this "decision" put me one step closer to my destiny?* (Replace "*decision*" with relationship, choice, habit, event, or whatever situation you may be facing.) If the decision is not aligned with your purpose, it's an easy no.
3. When you start to make decisions with your purpose in mind, choices become clear.
4. Everything you need to succeed is already within you.

Round 4

YOU'RE GOING TO GET KNOCKED OUT

"He who is in you is greater than he who is in the world."
–1 John 4:4 (NKJV)

It's time to grab your gear and prepare for battle. One of the most important aspects of preparing for a fight is understanding that your opponent's goal is to knock you out. To annihilate you. To make it the end of your story, or at least a chapter. You're being asked to embrace a series of unknowns as a fighter, but there is one thing you can be certain of: Your enemy's goal is to finish you. Understanding this concept is essential. Conversely, this is the same for you. You're the other opponent. When you engage in battle, your goal is to win. You want the result to be in your favor.

Your job is to prepare your mindset for battle. As a fighter on a path of purpose, you will, without question, come across many opponents. Your chances of getting kicked and punched exponentially increase. Think about it. When a fighter enters a ring or a cage, or even prepares for a fight, they expect to get hit. When an army goes to war, they put on protective equipment, flak vests, and helmets because they know there is a high probability that they'll get hit. Call it a preventative measure: protecting and preparing yourself are essential, not just to survive but to thrive. That is also the goal of your opponent. To think anything less would be naive.

You must adjust your mindset. As a fighter on a path of purpose, you're entering the ring daily and putting yourself in the crossfire. Real estate mogul Grant Cardone says, "If you're not experiencing fear, you're not pushing yourself enough."

Fear comes with entering the ring. We can watch videos to study our opponents and anticipate their next move. But there is always the unknown, the unpredictable, the chance of getting hit.

Embrace this mindset, accept this mindset, and choose to move forward despite the fear you're feeling. As a fighter with a purpose, you can be grounded in confidence and faith because you know who goes before you.

"And the LORD, He it is that doth go before thee; He will be with thee, He will not fail thee, neither forsake thee: fear not, neither be dismayed." (Deuteronomy 31:8)

"He who's greater in me than he who's of this world." (John 4:4) This is to say: Remember who's in your corner, guiding and directing you. Listen to your coach. This is your journey. This is what you signed up for. This is what you have "wrapped up" for. It's time to fight.

When we strive to max out our potential, to push through all limiting beliefs and labels and meet our highest self, we'll be confronted with fears, confusion, and challenges. When this happens, remind yourself that this is all part of the process. The seed never would have been planted if it were not a dream worth fighting for. I know this is easier said than done. It's not supposed to be easy.

In the midst of a fight, winning may seem impractical. Chances are high that you may at some point want to quit, throw in the towel, or raise that white flag. Hear this:

- It's supposed to be hard.
- It doesn't get easier. You get stronger. Quicker. Smarter.
- Victory is not won without blood, sweat, and tears.
- The scars, bruises, and pain all have meaning.

It will take more work, more time, and more sacrifice than ever before to level up. But also hear this:

- Everything you need to succeed is already within you.
- Every time you enter the ring, it's an opportunity to learn and grow.
- You will leave each battle more experienced and stronger than when you started.
- Don't give up. Don't throw in the towel. Remember who you are. You're a fighter.
- If you desire to become a champion to win that belt, you must consistently and persistently, without quitting, pursue your potential.
- With that desire comes challenges, trials, tests, and a lot of work.

The universe is going to test you. How bad do you really want it? It's during these battles that the good diminishes, and the great will rise. And the others? The average or below-average don't even show up to fight. Those are the victims, the complainers, the lazy, the individuals who usually have an excuse for everything. They immediately give up when faced with adversity. Don't be one of those people.

Throughout your journey, you will come across these types, and it will make you scratch your head. You will not quite understand why someone isn't willing to put in the work to save their dream and live their destiny. You're not meant to understand, because it doesn't make sense. Don't become a victim of your circumstances or what the universe may throw at you to test you. Suffering exposes a man or woman to their highest potential.

REMINDER: Suffering exposes a man or woman to their highest potential.

This is where champions emerge. The best will rise to the top. Those who are willing to work hard, not give up, and continue to pursue their potential, no matter the cost, will find victory. But how do we rise?

If you can look up, you can get up. You must get back up. When you feel like you cannot take another hit, or walk another step, or face another challenge, remember that adversity is necessary for optimal human development. Champions are not born; they're made. It's moments like these, the tests, where we go from ordinary to extraordinary. It's when our faith is tested. Faith untested cannot be trusted. Lean on this. Believe this.

Decide: I am reclaiming the power I have been given and moving forward with my mission.

Find Your Purpose

Easier said than done, right? Actually, it is. You have just been overcomplicating it. Here's what I have found: When you approach every chapter, every "round," and every battle in your life as an opportunity, your world will change.

What do I mean by that? As a fighter, you must be in a consistent and constant pursuit of your potential. You come from greatness. Greatness is within you. You *are* greatness, and you must *be* greatness. This means giving 100 percent to any situation you're chosen to be a part of.

Every day is an opportunity. Tomorrow is not guaranteed, so why would you not live today as if it were an opportunity? That means, even when taking out the trash, it's done with purpose. It's selfish and downright lazy to perform at any level less than 100 percent. I want you to be an example of living with such enthusiasm and gratitude that your kids see your example and want the opportunity to add "take out trash" to their chore list.

My biggest motivator every day is to pursue my potential. I look forward to the day that I get to meet my Lord and Savior, when he recognizes me as the woman he created me to be. We're all created for a purpose, and that is to pursue our full potential. And we all have gifts that make us uniquely who we are. Gifts that we're meant to explore and help others benefit from. Your purpose is to find these gifts that are unique to you and give them away in the form of service to others. The rent is due every day for our stay here on Earth, and it's paid through service to others.

When your mindset shifts from "I have to do something" to "I *get* to do something" (fill in the blank), your world will start to evolve. As a fighter and as a leader, you cannot call it in or do a half-ass job. Approaching life with a ho-hum attitude isn't acceptable. Champions claim titles and hold titles because of their ability to be in constant pursuit of their potential, no matter the situation, circumstance, or challenge that they may find themselves in.

There will be jobs you don't like and would rather not do, and supervisors whom you don't understand and dislike. There will be situations and circumstances that you could really care less about. There will be challenges that require you to get in the ring and fight when you would rather be Netflixing or chilling with your friends. But it doesn't matter. Your circumstances and feelings at the time don't change your DNA. You're a champion in the making, and how you approach these situations will determine if you move closer to your destiny or farther away. Will you tap out? Or will you choose to continue to accept what you're called upon to become?

Whatever task you're given, whatever job you may hold, whatever role you may be playing in this chapter you find yourself in, you must approach it with purpose. You must resolve to give 100 percent of your abilities and talents to the situation. You will show up and put up not just a good fight, but a great fight. Because remember, the good eventually fall, but the great will rise.

Every day is an opportunity to chase the destiny version of you. The present, the here and now, is a gift. How will you make the most of it?

Fighters exceed expectations. Fighters choose not just to go the extra mile, but the "empty mile." The extra mile isn't consistently attained. The empty mile, however, is where you're consistently showing up as a champion. This is definitely a road less traveled.

"For wide is the gate and broad is the road that leads to destruction, and many enter through it. But small is the gate and narrow the road that leads to life, and only a few find it."
–Matthew 7:13-14

Champions show up early, stay late, and do whatever it takes to get the job done, and they do it well. There isn't a 9 a.m. to 5 p.m. "warrior's clock-out" on the day's job and mission. It becomes so simple once you understand the concept that *this is a lifestyle.*

When you approach rounds in life with the mindset that you will be in constant pursuit of your potential, the universe rewards you with more. You will not level up until you have paid your dues in your current chapter or battle. Goals and milestones will not be achieved until you're able to master the level where you're at. What are you willing to sacrifice in the short term for your long-term goals? It starts with deciding. Are you ready to take that step?

Start by applying purpose *now*. Wherever you're at in your journey, this chapter deserves the best version of you. Anything less than your best is a disservice to yourself and those around you. Anything less than your best is not congruent with a fighter's mentality. Remind yourself who you are and what is in your DNA. You're a warrior. There is no backing down, ever.

Stop approaching life as if it's *happening* to you. You play the lead role in your story. You hold the pen that writes that next sentence or scene. You get to determine the outcome. How will this chapter end? You get to decide how to defend yourself and fight back. No matter how bad the situation may be right now, embrace the suck. Reframe that suck into an opportunity to advance. Fight for it. Remember that you're a fighter. Your purpose is to max out your potential, learn, and grow. You're a champion in the making.

Discover what talents and gifts you have been blessed with, and then share them with the world. What are your strengths? How can you use them to serve others? We all have what I call a "superpower." This is a gift or strength, something you're good at and enjoy doing, your greatness within, so to speak.

The number one gift I have been blessed with is the ability to help others discover their own superpowers and to help them develop and maximize their potential. With this comes my ability to build incredible teams that harmonize well and maximize efficiency and potential.

My second gift is my ability to create systems. I can take a business or organization and help build systems that provide structure, continuity, and efficiency. And most importantly, duplicability. This allows ordinary people to have extraordinary results. I can see the bigger picture, the vision, and create a harmony within an organization that's music to your ears.

My third gift is my ability to emotionally connect, feel, and empathize with other people. In less than five minutes, I am able to feel their energy and build a rapport, so they trust me enough to open up to me. This is powerful in my mission to connect with individuals, helping them maximize their potential and shine.

What about you? What are your gifts? What do you do well and enjoy doing? What would you do whether or not you were getting paid?

Your purpose will never change. Your mission, however, will change depending on your current chapter. But your purpose, never. As fighters, we're required to perform at a certain level. We're required to put on our gloves, get in the ring, and fight. We must be willing to solve problems and be next-level thinkers. You don't have to be the smartest person in the room. In fact, if you are, you should probably find another room. Without question, though, you should be willing to outwork anyone in that room. When connected to our purpose, with our mission in mind, if we get knocked down, we automatically have the inspiration to get back up and fight.

Visualize It

Are you a wandering generality? Or are you a meaningful specific? My once-dear friend and mentor, Zig Ziglar, may he rest in peace, reminds us, "You were born to win, but to be a winner you must plan to win, prepare to win, and expect to win."

What are you expecting? What is your vision? Your bigger reason? The "why" that drives everything you do? The reason you walk into that ring each day with your chest pressed out, shoulders pulled back, and head held high. What keeps you marching into battle after battle with confidence and strength?

We have daily, weekly, monthly, and even long-term goals that extend out five to ten years. Goals are important, and they should be set and assessed often. But what I am asking you to do is stop for a moment and think even bigger. What's going to keep you in the ring when you're taking hits left and right, sucker punches, and knockouts?

What do you want your life to look and feel like? Your vision must include big, hairy, audacious goals (a.k.a. BHAG), as Jim Collins points out in his book, *Good to Great*. These goals must be so big that your friends and family think you're crazy. These goals should scare you and excite you at the same time. They should scare you because you know you will need to embrace discomfort to reach them, but excite you because of the person you will become once you master them. The feeling should be so intense that when you think about it, you tear up. As you construct this vision about what your life will look and feel like and the things you can do for your family and this world, the desire to push beyond your perceived limits is reinforced.

Money matters. What you can do with money matters. Whether it's giving the best to the ones you love or the organizations that you want to help, money is the energy that accomplishes just that. If you believe you're thinking big, chances are you're not thinking big enough. I used to believe I thought big and that money did not matter. But it does. Money is not the motivator, but what you can do with that money motivates and drives you to dream, build bigger, and push past roadblocks.

I want you to stretch your imagination far out of your comfort zone. Kind of like those yoga positions you see where your jaw drops because you just cannot figure out how they got their legs in that position. Become that uncomfortable.

When I left high school to join the military, it was because of a bigger vision I had for myself and my family. I did not want to continue the cycle my family was in; the generational curse of poverty-level income had to come to an end. I did not want to live paycheck to paycheck, and I wanted to provide more for my family. I saw how hard my mother worked, and I watched daily as she sacrificed to provide just the minimum for us. I wanted to get out of the neighborhood where you were afraid to walk alone at night or even during the day. I wanted to provide more for my family, not just the needs but also the wants: the vacations and the dinners out that weren't at fast food restaurants. I didn't want to have to buy at secondhand stores or shop with WIC checks or live where someone told me I had to, because that's where I "belonged."

Upon finding myself divorced yet again after my mother's passing, I feared falling into old family patterns and poverty. The vision I described earlier burned so deeply in my soul that it transformed me into this superhuman. It became the driving force behind my 4 a.m. wakeups to build a fitness bootcamp business in the park across the street from my house. I then followed that with a ten-hour day as an education consultant at a college. I would then do all the things required of a parent: pick up the kids from school, help them with their homework, cook dinner, and do chores around the house. After putting my angels to bed, I'd then buckle down to complete my own homework. I was also a full-time student pursuing a degree in business management.

My days were long, nights even longer. And I was fueled by coffee, 5-Hour Energy drinks, and a strong vision. I was running on little sleep but a massive dream. I was willing and ready to do whatever it took to push forward. It's amazing what you become capable of when your vision is so vivid in your mind.

Some might say, and I did hear it often: "Melissa, that is a lot on your plate. Why don't you slow down?" I could have played the victim. I would be lying if I didn't acknowledge the days that I lay in bed a bit too long and cried and asked, "Why me?" But my desire, my dream, and my vision outweighed my discomfort and pain. The deep gnawing in my soul told me to move with conviction toward the destiny God had fixed in place long before the fight began.

Understand this: Success loves speed. Champions don't slow down. We don't downgrade our dreams to fit our reality. We upgrade our conviction to match our destiny. When you ask to be fed like a champion, don't complain about how much is on your plate. Embrace the suck, enjoy the journey, and be thankful for your wonderfully chaotic world.

REMINDER: Ignoring or avoiding your destiny in the short term will only cause you pain in the long term.

Although my first-grade teacher labeled me "average," I still worked hard, and I had a consistent desire to exceed standard norms. I'd do my best to be my best, confront challenges, and strive for more. My senior year in high school lit a fire in my soul and helped facilitate the restructuring of my core beliefs about myself and about the world. Believing that I could become whatever I put my mind to and was willing to work hard for, magically opened doors for me.

One of those doors was the military. It was there that I was able to exceed expectations and perform at a level that proved to be rewarding and exhilarating. I felt in control of my destiny. Although I think we all know, in the military, you will always have someone dictating what you can or cannot do, regardless of your rank or position.

Even the President of the United States has someone to keep him in check and balanced. I appreciated the opportunity to compete against my peers and standards and to be recognized and rewarded for my efforts and determination. I'd always complete tasks and missions in record time. And I often found myself improving the processes and systems. I was promoted early and advanced into positions that were created for high performers because of my diligence and determination.

The confidence that I built in the military poured over into my civilian world after separation. I enjoyed the positions I had the opportunity to be a part of, like being an education consultant. I learned new skills. It was challenging, and it provided security through a guaranteed paycheck. However, I found myself quickly surpassing my peers, creating and conquering systems, starting new programs, and exchanging time for money. I was rewarded for my work in the civilian sector, but there were limits and ceilings that I could not break through, even though I knew I was capable of more. This was when I realized clocking into someone else's agenda and dream was not for me.

Have you ever been in a position where you knew there had to be more? Both careers I just referenced, as an airman in the USAF and as an education consultant, were quality careers. And both played an important role in my story and in building my character. But I knew deep down there was something else out there that was much bigger with my name on it.

There is significance as well for you in the chapter you're currently writing. There are lessons to be extracted. There is purpose behind the punches you're taking. You may not be able to connect the dots now or even understand what role this position will play in your future, but know that there is a reason for the season you're in. The bigger picture may be a bit blurry, but it will eventually come into focus. I encourage you to continue to hold the pen, or take back the pen, and write your story. Get in the ring and fight like the champion your destiny requires.

What is your "why"? Can you visualize it? Can you believe it? How does it feel? Does it hurt when you think about not achieving it? If you cannot answer any of these questions, you need to dig deeper.

The Traits Of A Fighter

Your purpose, mission, and values will keep you in the ring of life, fighting the battles with strength and determination, when the odds are against you and you feel like the underdog. You must clearly define your purpose, mission, and values. We have discussed your purpose and your mission; now we'll touch on the glue that holds them together, and that's the foundation of values. The values you choose to live by and make decisions with will guide you as you go into battle. When you have clearly defined values, making decisions becomes a lot simpler. The idea here is not to be a wandering generality, but a fighter with standards that you uphold. I have four core values that I live by:

- Excellence in all I do

- Servant Leadership
- Discipline
- Gratitude

Excellence in all I do is a value I adopted from the military. It was the first time I was introduced to the power behind having set values. No matter the job, regardless of how shitty the conditions or situation or how I may have felt that day, I was required to show up 100 percent of the time and give 100 percent.

In the military, this core value holds great significance. How you show up as a warrior daily impacts not just you, but your fellow comrades and the mission. We were all responsible for accomplishing that day's objectives and long-term ones as well. Lives were at stake; our beloved country and the freedoms we hold dearly were all on the line. This instilled in me a strong work ethic that I carry with me to this day.

I was in Iraq, serving in Operation Enduring Freedom, supporting an F-16 unit as a work group manager. I assisted in the setup of the computer systems and network on the base, as well as a variety of other tasks. We all had multiple duties in the military. It was a mentality of "Do what needs to be done" to stay functional and war-ready. We worked 12-hour shifts every day, in 100-plus-degree weather, in full gear, including Kevlar vests and helmets. There wasn't air conditioning; we used porta johns, slept in tents, used bottled water for brushing our teeth, and walked at least a mile for a five-minute cold shower. We even had the almost daily mortar attacks to keep us on our toes. The situation sucked. Like, capital SUCKED. But that did not change the way we operated or our core value of excellence in all we did. Whatever was needed to accomplish the mission, we always put forth our best effort.

REMINDER: How you do anything is how you do everything.

To give anything less than your best is a waste of time and energy. Why participate in something or sign your name on a task or job if you're only going to give it a portion of your ability? This falls right in line with a fighter's purpose to be in consistent pursuit of the best version of you. Aim for champion status.

* * *

Servant leadership, or as I was taught in the Air Force, "service before self," is another core value that continues to guide my daily actions. I have always felt good serving. In fact, when I feel depressed, overwhelmed, or down on my luck, my first thought is to serve. It's very difficult to have any sort of negative feeling when you're giving back. HINT: This is a system or tool that you should adopt and use often. In the military, the mission always came first. I watched as my mother put my siblings and me before herself. And the greatest of all examples of servant leadership is Jesus.

It's one thing to serve, and it's another dimension entirely to serve your organization or people. When you lead from a servant's mentality, "How can I help you?" versus "What can you do for me?" you attract and build an alternate reality. This is another massive lesson that I operate and function from daily. It was also a lesson that took me years to hear, comprehend, and master completely. However, when I heard it, accepted it, and understood the power behind it, my reality was forever altered. I found clarity and peace. I operated and led not out of fear or expectation, but out of love and grace, questioning less and accepting more.

To love and lead without expectation places you in a position of peace. It's difficult to be let down by someone or something if you don't expect anything to begin with. It forces you to lead from a place of acceptance and understanding. I am, without a doubt, convinced that my mission is to love and lead like Jesus did. It's so rare in the world that when you do come across it or experience it, you question motives, and mine have been questioned often. It's difficult for some individuals to understand that someone can do something for another without expecting anything in return. That, to me, is a relationship with conditions attached.

The Prayer of Jabez is a story and prayer that continues to greatly impact my life. It resonates with me deeply and is the foundation behind my life's mission: ***"Oh that you would bless me indeed. And enlarge my territory. That you would keep me from evil. That I may not cause pain."*** **(1 Chronicles 4:10)**

Jabez is asking God to bless him abundantly. To give abundantly and serve in abundance. We also need to receive in abundance. Eradicate yourself of a scarcity mindset. We're the children of the Most High God who created the heavens and the earth. He is more than capable and qualified to provide for you and the purpose he needs you to fulfill. When I am in doubt of my ability to serve on a higher level, on a massive scale, or when I am presented with an opportunity that may seem unbelievable, I simply remind myself that it's not about me. It's about what he can do through me. My rent on earth is paid through serving others. Zig Ziglar also reiterates this point: "You can have everything you want in life if you will just help other people get what they want."

Whether you believe in God or another higher being, understand that we live in an abundant universe. And having an abundant mindset, where there is enough for everyone as long as you're willing to put in the work to get it, will transform the way you operate and receive.

* * *

Discipline is the battery that fuels the values of servant leadership and excellence in all that I do. Being disciplined requires hard work. Another value I adopted from my military tenure is discipline, which all fighters must adopt as part of their lifestyle. Discipline will set the foundation for everything else you do or don't want to do. To be relentlessly disciplined is a trait champions strive to uphold daily. When you build a lifestyle based on discipline, your world will flow regardless of your circumstances.

In the military, during basic training, one of the first values they teach you is discipline. It's taught through a series of routines, processes, and habits you must follow. Discipline requires the desire to serve a bigger mission. Discipline makes establishing this habit and instilling this value very simple. When the mission is to either protect or save lives, then following procedure is a must. Therefore, it's very important to understand and form your mission and purpose. When you fully comprehend what it is you're fighting for, establishing the habits necessary to accomplish the mission becomes simple. Again, simple, not easy. But it becomes much simpler once you understand that it requires discipline backed by habits that serve your mission.

I was first introduced to the power of simple daily disciplines fresh out of the Air Force when I joined my first network marketing company.

There is a natural progression in life: first, you must plant, then cultivate, and then harvest. Small disciplines compounded over time produce massive results. These disciplines or habits can also make or break you. The right disciplines, like working out daily, reading ten pages of a book that enhances your world, and eating a well-balanced, nutrient-dense diet, compounded over time, have a significant impact.

Likewise, if you don't work out every day and eat processed food consistently, you may not notice any significant life-altering changes for the first week or month. But over time, compounded, these bad habits will have a significant detrimental impact. Luckily for you and me, we get to choose our habits. Change your habits, change your life.

* * *

Gratitude: I grew up being taught to say "please" and "thank you," and I always had a sense of appreciation. But I lived very much in a scarcity mindset after leaving home at eighteen. I grew up in a land of "not enough." I was determined to get to a place of "just enough" and honestly could not wrap my mind around ever having "more than enough." Because of this upbringing, I was immensely grateful for whatever I had and was determined to earn more.

"Change the way you look at things, and the things you look at change."

–Wayne Dyer

When you're stripped of what you believe gives meaning to your life, when you feel that there is nothing left that gives your life meaning, you start to reevaluate what you give value to. This was the case for me. My mission was to provide for my mother. I missed the mark. It was at that moment that I became grateful for minutes and moments. I finally found value in not just the "not enough," but the money and all the things money could buy. What I realized was that there was a more abundant world out there than the one I lived in. I had life. I had a purpose.

Gratitude reconnects us to our Source. When you come to understand that every day you wake up with a heartbeat is something to be grateful for, and all that follows is the cherry on top, you move differently. You think differently. You're grateful for challenges, trials, people, light, and air! Everything matters, and nothing matters at all. Grateful.

With gratitude, you will effortlessly instill the other three values: service before self, servant leadership, and discipline. It's the binder of all that is necessary to live a life of purpose.

Your job is to prepare your mindset for battle. Master your mind, and you will ultimately win the battle every time. As a fighter on a path of purpose, you will, without question, come across many opponents. You will get knocked down, you will take hits, and you will face adversity. This is all part of your journey. This journey, this fight for the title, becomes a lot simpler if you enter the ring with a solid understanding of your purpose. Your confidence will increase because it's built on a solid foundation of your vision and values.

What are your values? Adopt mine if you'd like. I borrowed them and made them my own. But understand this: your purpose, mission, and values are your operational guide. You will not function at your highest level without them.

ROUND 4 TAKEAWAYS

1. *"He who is in me is greater than he who is in the world."* (1 John 4:4)
2. Suffering exposes a man or woman to their highest potential.
3. Faith untested can't be trusted.
4. Ignoring or avoiding your destiny only causes you pain.
5. Your purpose, mission, and values are your operational guide. You will not function at your highest level without them. Take some time now to draft your mission, purpose, and values.

My mission:

____

____

____

My purpose:

____

____

____

My values:

____

____

____

Round 5

HAVE YOUR CORNER COVERED

"You're the average of the five people you associate with most."
–Jim Rohn

Let it sink in for a moment: "You're the average of the five people you associate with most." Who do you allow in your circle? Take an inventory of the people who are closest to you: friends, coworkers, and family members. Who do you spend most of your time with?

Now, recall your vision. Your goals. Your mission. Your values. Your identity. Are those people you listed helping or hurting you? Are they adding to your life or taking away from it? Are they a positive or negative influence on you?

As a fighter, a champion in the making, you will need to regularly take inventory of your associations. You will need to remove individuals from your circle who don't align with your vision, mission, values, goals, and identity. I know this sounds harsh, but I am not here to sell you on easy. This is one of the best decisions you can make for yourself. You may need to start limiting contact with a family member. I call it "loving them from a distance." Pray for them and move on; then be who you are. Toxic relationships will keep you from performing at your full potential; they will drain your energy, have you operating at a low frequency, knock you off course, and make it take you longer to reach your goals, if you end up reaching them at all. They will become distractions on your way to your destiny.

The fights, battles, and challenges you find yourself most often involved in will be between you and the individuals who are not aligned with where you want to be or where you're going. Deep down, you know you're meant for more. But when you're associated with individuals who don't align with your vision, you tend to attract similar qualities. Are they lazy, unmotivated, and content with the status quo? Are they just drifting through life as a wandering generality? Do they have habits that are not aligned with a fighter's lifestyle, like bad eating habits, smoking, heavy drinking, and excessive partying, such that they don't live a healthy lifestyle? When you allow these individuals in your sphere, you'll adopt (probably unconsciously) the same characteristics in order to get along or feel camaraderie with them. Closely monitor who's in your circle, inventory often, and quickly remove anyone who's not on a similar path as yourself. You owe it to yourself to be your best by being surrounded by the best.

Get A Coach

Who's wrapping your hands? Who's there in your corner of the ring, coaching you through your fight? As a fighter, you don't have an option: you must have a coach and/or a mentor.

Recall this statement: "You're the average of the five people you associate with most." Are you around and associating with people you want to be like? It bears repeating: If you're the smartest person in the room, I encourage you to find a new room. As fighters and champions in the making, you need to be consistently pursuing your potential. The best way to do this is to learn from those who've already been where you want to go. Not only will you learn from them, but you'll increase your rate of success. It's seriously a time saver! Your growth will be exponentially impacted. What would have taken you ten years will now take you only two, because you're learning from others who have already made the mistakes and been there, done that.

Coaches and mentors are an investment in yourself, just like your education. Some people will pay for an education that teaches them a trade or for a college education that they won't even use. But when it comes to investing in mentors and coaches who will teach them how to get to that next level, they tend to second-guess the decision and the expense.

I was first introduced to mentors when I was in the military. One of the biggest lessons I took from the service is the necessity to "train to replace," meaning that, in the military, you always train your subordinates to replace you. We're always building for the next position, rank, or promotion. I had a couple of decent supervisors and, well, some others who weren't. You were trained to do your job, and possibly theirs eventually, but there was occasionally some sense of jealousy or resentment.

A true leader trains to replace, knowing that they will also replace the next position up. A leader has a responsibility to build leaders. I worked hard in the military. Always above and beyond. It never crossed my mind to give anything less than my best. Thinking back, I was probably copying my mother's work ethic.

I quickly climbed to a position as the Command Chief's Executive Assistant. It was a highly visible position that supported the multiple squadrons or units that make up a wing. And it could only be filled by a recommendation. It was a great position for me, very busy and challenging, and it gave me access to Chief Sanders. He was the type of individual who led by example, provided opportunities for growth, and poured knowledge into his airmen. He became a mentor to me at no cost, except for my willingness to learn and grow.

This kind of mentorship translates directly to the civilian world, for pouring knowledge into others and accomplishing the mission. You cannot be afraid to empower and develop your team. The better you take care of them, the better they will take care of your business.

Additionally, those of us blessed to be in a leadership position have a responsibility to coach and mentor others. Get it out of your head that someone might be out to get you. That's a scarcity mindset creeping up on you. Where it may seem they just might be "in that ring to take you out," I promise you, the more you focus on your growth and development and helping those around you to do the same, you will outwork, out-think, and outgrow your opponents!

REMINDER: We live in an abundant universe. Give and receive!

But Melissa, I cannot afford a mentor… I know some of you are thinking this. First, I say, "Stop your stinking thinking." Chief Sanders would often say that. Second, I'd tell you that I didn't pay for some of my mentors, or not an excessive amount, anyway. Your mentors may come in the form of books and podcasts. Podcasts are free, and books require a very minimal investment. Or better yet, head over to your public library. The amount of personal development and coaching I have received from books is astronomical. I often read these books, thinking to myself: *Man, I can't wait to meet this person one day,* or, *Wow! Maybe I could be mentored or coached by this person one day.*

I would seek out opportunities to meet these individuals, including Zig Ziglar, Les Brown, Bob Burg, Jeff Olson, Brian Tracy, Mel Robbins, Bedros Keullian, and David Meltzer, to name a few. With all of these individuals, I would first read their books or listen to their podcasts. They were my mentors, my guides, and an intrinsic part of who I have become, continue to become, and level up with. I saved up money to take trips to see these legends at seminars and conferences. While my peers were partying and buying the next purse or vehicle, I was in the front-row seat, investing in myself and my empire. There is power in proximity.

I have invested, and continue to invest, in myself through books and podcasts with simple daily disciplines: ten pages a day in a book and thirty minutes of a podcast. And I also invest in coaches, paying to have knowledgeable friends in my inner circle. It's a goal of mine to find myself in rooms with individuals more successful than I am.

Ask, and you shall receive. Act and you will become. Whatever way you want to put it, the more I invested in myself, the more I studied, and the more I became the person I wanted to be, the more I attracted similarly successful people into my circle. Not a coincidence. The frequency at which you operate in life and business is what you frequently see in others and attracts them to you. I had wealthy entrepreneurs coming to me, wanting to help me. Individuals on a similar path or journey who understood my goals and ambitions. Intention plus attention creates the coincidences in your life. There is no such thing as luck. When you prepare, and the opportunity shows itself, are you ready to bounce on it? Are you preparing accordingly?

Visualize this: You're in the ring; your opponent is across from you. Who's wrapping your hands? Who's standing in your corner? Who has coached and prepared you for the fight you're about to participate in? Recall those five closest associations. Who are you allowing in your inner circle? Just like a mother protecting her children, a lion protecting her cubs, you must protect your circle! Guard it. And inventory it often. Yes, there will be times when you go to inventory your associations, and there will be people you've outgrown. Individuals who have chosen to stay where they are in their comfort zone. I am not saying to rid yourself of friends and family. Rather, I am saying it's going to be a lot more difficult to get where you want to go if your tribe isn't headed in the same direction. You'll consistently get pulled back into old habits, patterns, and a lifestyle that do not align with your vision. Guard your vision, your destiny, and your dreams, and never apologize for them.

Have Your Corner Covered

As a champion, I want to be able to arrive at every fight as prepared as possible and ready to win. We've already determined that you will be in the ring fighting, so why not make sure the odds are in your favor?

I have set the foundation for my success in simple terms. I have mentors who cover the major portions of what I call the "pillars to success in my world": spiritual or faith, business (finances or career), and whatever specialty I am focused on.

* * *

Spiritual: I have a mentor who pours into me spiritually. As a fighter, you will be attacked. Spiritually connected individuals are constantly attacked by spiritual warfare. Having a mentor who can pray with and for you is a must. This individual also understands your connection to whatever your Higher Power is or your relationship with the universe.

The best mentor you can have in your corner, or in this area, is God. Be in consistent communication with him. This should be a no-brainer. But believe me, I understand. As a Type-A personality, leader, and someone who is sometimes hardheaded, I'll get stuck or simply forget that God is on my side. Most importantly, all I do is for him through me. It's his plan. So why wouldn't you be in consistent communication and connection with your Leader, your "right-hand Man," so to speak?

Personally, this is my foundation. I start my day with this Coach and Mentor. He is first. It's his plan, and his purpose for me. So, I dive deep into his word every morning. I call it "God's time" on my calendar. I journal, pray, meditate, and listen to gospel music. No coincidences, right? But I have noticed that if I forget this element of my daily routine because I'm too busy to connect first thing, the rest of my day seems out of alignment.

I challenge you to align your day with his purpose by starting off in prayer and in his word. Start with "the Man with the plan."

* * *

Business: I am building an empire. I haven't built one before. There are plenty of others who have. Being mentored by individuals who have taken businesses to where I want to take mine is a must for me. They have made the mistakes; they know the better options. It's about letting go of your ego and allowing others to help and guide you. You don't know what you don't know. With a mentor, you'll get there so much quicker. Having those outside eyes looking in will catch things you're not aware of. Additionally, seek mentors who are in your same area of expertise as well as others who are not. It's beneficial to surround yourself with variety; this can add a fresh perspective. It also provides an enormous learning opportunity into other possible fields of future interest.

* * *

Your Specialty: What is your focus? Is it consulting? Marketing? Coaching? Is it a product or service? There are so many specialties out there. Find someone who's doing what you want to do, but doing it better. Who's where you want to be? Go learn from them.

I often get asked, "What book would you recommend?" My answer usually is: "Well, what are you striving to become?" Find books that focus on it. Find podcasts that focus on it. Do that and become one of the best in your field.

Never stop learning. And know you'll never be the best; someone will always be better. But find a way to continue to be a better you. You can't stop learning and growing as a champion. When you enter that battlefield, you need to be able to outsmart your opponent. To do that, align yourself with an individual who has been through similar battles.

Now, I know that seems like a lot. But if you counted, that is three mentors. Three pillars. Three individuals in my circle of five. These three individuals pour into me daily. What is most remarkable about this situation is that I didn't find all three of them at once. As I started to build my empire, I felt like something was missing. And I realized I needed guidance in certain areas. Understanding the power of influence and mentors, I'd ask the universe to place someone in my path to guide me.

Individuals who become your mentors will be in your life for seasons. They will also change as you grow and develop your life. They'll come and go.

You attract what you are or what you are becoming. You attract your energy. If your energy is consistent and persistent in pursuit of all that you can become, you'll attract like-minded individuals. That is the only way I can explain it. Be careful, though, because the opposite is also true. If you're not attracting who you want, you may need to look in the mirror and ask yourself, *Who do I want to be around to help me? What energy am I exuding? Am I giving what I want to receive?* Self-inventory your habits, values, and goals; adjust, then proceed.

I have multiple powerhouses, empire builders, and incredibly successful entrepreneurs and leaders who pour knowledge into me daily. I have access to them because I made the choice, did the work, and showed up. Never forget: "You're the average of the five people you associate with most." Be careful who you choose.

My mentors and coaches don't stop there. I know we may not always have access to individuals in the flesh. I've paid good money for many of my mentors. Paid for my knowledgeable friends. Invested in myself through others. I've invested more in mentors and coaches than I have in my college education, and I hold a master's degree, folks, but the level of education you'll receive from a coach and mentor far exceeds an advanced education. It's real-life training.

Your Environment

Review your environment. As fighters, we need to be able to perform at a high level. If you're largely consuming network television, Netflix, or the news, ask yourself, *Is this helping me reach my potential and in alignment with my vision and purpose?* I'm sure you've heard the saying "garbage in, garbage out." Take an inventory of everything within ten feet of you. The news is so negative, and most of what's on TV is a time suck. What are you listening to? What are you watching? What's in your pantry? We need to make conscious decisions. What's within your reach?

More often than not, I hear the excuse, "I don't have time." This isn't a time management issue; it's a time integrity issue. How are you really spending your time? I picked up a time hack from a mentor of mine, "Ace" Fair, who came up with "Drive Time University." Drive Time University is exactly what it sounds like: Learning while you drive. Most of us spend a good amount of time commuting to work. Even if it's not a lot, ten minutes there and back, or while in the car running errands or on trips. These are opportunities to invest in yourself. I started with CDs and audiobooks. I am talking about self-help books that enhance your skills personally and professionally, not *Harry Potter* or a romance novel. Ask yourself, *Will what I am listening to help me level up?*

At the time, Ace was my mentor in a direct-selling business called Pre-Paid Legal. This was one of my first "jobs" outside of the Air Force. What I learned from direct selling, network marketing, and Ace and his wife, Gina, has helped to mold a big part of who I am. This company introduced me to personal development.

One of the first books I read, by an individual I was blessed to meet, was *The Slight Edge* by Jeff Olson. This book teaches the concept that small daily habits will either make or break you. The actions and habits we perform daily will either keep us on the success curve or send us in the opposite direction. They may not be noticeable at the time, but literally, they will shape your future.

I could easily knock out ten minutes listening to an audiobook or a podcast, a habit I still maintain a decade later. I can read ten pages of a book a day. Compounded over time, these habits have a massive impact. You get to decide what your habits are. Choose wisely.

I haven't always had the funds to pay for a mentor. My mentoring started with books, podcasts, and attending the occasional event where these individuals were speaking. I still do this. You get access to these individuals, and then, thank goodness for social media, you have even more access to them. There is no excuse. Get a mentor, or three or four. Invest in who you want to become.

Sorting Through it All

Create a routine. This is so important for those wanting to rise above the status quo. There is so much information out there that we can easily drown in it every day; therefore, you need to have a plan. Becoming the best and building an empire requires habits that average people don't have. You must consume content daily that will help keep you in a state of positive flow. This consumption of positive, fulfilling information will assist in the production not only of yourself but also of your income and impact.

There is a ton of information out there. Choose a few to start. I call it "building your perfect mentor." Find those individuals who best align with your values and mission; stick with three. Then consume their information in the form of books, podcasts, events, etc.

For example, when I wake up in the morning, I read from a specific book. This is usually more spiritually related; it reminds me of my overall purpose and who's on my side (wink). Just a few pages, but this sets the tone for the day and gives me something to ponder throughout my workout and my day. I then listen to a podcast while showering. This usually concerns productivity and coaching for my business. It helps to get me even more into the right mindset to tackle the day, and it also educates me. While I am driving, I typically listen to Christian music or spiritual podcasts. This continues to keep me in the right heart-set.

I am protective of my social media time. The only individuals I follow are those who, you guessed it, are doing what I want to do or have similar values. My social media accounts are literally personal development reels. I'll also dedicate at least fifty minutes a day to studying research, one of my mentors, or areas I need to develop. Finally, in the evening, it's ten more pages of reading before I call it a night.

You see, we all have time; you just have to first decide what your priorities are. Then you must *start*, and you must *ask* for help. This will transform your world. But you need to act and have initiative. Create a plan, then follow through with discipline. Model what is already there.

Seek and utilize the resources and tools that are already being used by the people who are crushing it in your industry or field of expertise. I promise you, most of the people doing it already didn't get to where they are without a tribe, without a team, without mentors pouring into them. If they didn't have their corner covered, someone wrapping their hands and wiping the sweat off their face, or someone telling them to get back up and that they can do it when they get knocked down, they would not be where they are today.

Do it.

ROUND 5 TAKEAWAYS:

1. Small daily habits compounded over time will either make or break you. What is a habit you can acquire right now that will keep you in alignment with your goals?
2. You're the average of the five people you associate with most. Write down your closest five. Who are "keepers?" Who do you need to remove? Who can you replace them with?
3. You're in the ring, your opponent across from you. Who's wrapping your hands, and who's standing in your corner? Who's your mentor(s)?

Round 6

YOUR FIGHTER STANCE

"For I know the plans I have for you," declares the LORD, "plans to prosper you and not to harm you, plans to give you hope and a future."
–Jeremiah 29:11 (NIV)

Resilience is a measure of how much you want something and how much you're willing and able to overcome obstacles to get it. It has everything to do with your emotional strength. Just like servant leadership and excellence, resiliency is a "muscle" that must be worked and developed. You must be able to put yourself in situations that push you out of your comfort zone, and do not quit. You must get in the ring, you must develop your resilience, and you must be willing to get hit. A true fighter knows this and prepares for it accordingly.

Resilience is also commonly paired with mental toughness. When stepping into the ring of life as a fighter, you will be subjected to more trials and challenges than most; you will be tested and confronted with demons. On your journey to level up and make an impact on a massive scale, you will inevitably be hit with setbacks, barriers, and sucker punches. For this reason, you must attack life as a warrior with the correct mindset. You must be willing and ready to overcome any obstacle that places itself in your path. Understanding and accepting that you will face battles is the first step in overcoming these challenges.

Having resilience means that challenges no longer come as a surprise to you; they're all part of the game or the bigger plan on the journey to your destination. However, during this journey, the second step you must master is activating your fighter stance and being prepared to defend your mission and fight back. Getting into your fighter stance without hesitation will save you time and pain and reduce the damage you take.

Knowing your fighter stance and how to get there quickly is a technique all fighters must master and implement automatically when life throws punches and kicks. The importance of being able to activate this stance efficiently and effectively in your life determines how quickly you can recover from life's challenges, trials, and punches. Initiating your fighter stance when an attack is imminent arms you with confidence and strength. It puts you in a fighter's mentality. You're ready to go to war.

It's absolutely guaranteed that you will be hit. As a leader, a champion in the making, living out your purpose and fulfilling your destiny, the chances of you being hit will increase. However, if you're able to activate your fighter stance, you will prevail. In fact, as you strengthen your resiliency muscle, you'll notice that, although life's challenges don't slow down, you can better navigate these storms and hits because of the resiliency you have built.

Life will start to get into a state of flow. At first, when I entered this state of flow, it almost felt like I was doing something wrong because it was so unfamiliar compared to my previous state of operation. I previously operated in fear and lived in a scarcity mindset. When you shift your focus to a state of faith, courage, abundance, and purpose, you'll find an incredible sense of peace. You're so mentally prepared and in such a zone of awareness and focus that you no longer move to the world's beat; rather, the world moves to your beat. You're the narrator and the star in your show. (More on this in a later chapter.)

Your fighter stance represents a confident, purpose-driven, fearless individual. This is your new mindset. A fighter's mindset.

Napoleon Hill, in his incredible book, *Outwitting the Devil,* talks about the power of being fearless:

> Fear is the tool of a man-made devil. Self-confident faith in oneself is both the man-made weapon that defeats the devil and the man-made tool that builds a triumphant life. And it is more than that. It is a link to irresistible forces of the universe, which stand behind a man who does not believe in failure and defeat as being anything but temporary experiences.

You're able to overcome *fear* for three main reasons:

1. You tell yourself that you have a life mission and God, your Silent Partner, who's accessible at any moment you choose. Remind yourself that you have a purpose bigger than you can imagine and a force that goes before you.

2. You're resilient and have prepared for these moments; all the tools you need to win these battles are within you.

3. You understand that failure and defeat are just temporary experiences; that you will learn and become better from this

attempted attack on the journey to your destiny. Like Sir Winston Churchill said, "Success is tumbling from failure to failure with no loss of enthusiasm."

The Power of Systems and Implementing Them

My first real job was at McDonald's. At the age of fourteen, I started working part-time throughout high school to contribute to my family's income and to be able to provide myself with some of the stuff the "cool kids" had in school. My mother couldn't afford anything but the basics; it was usually hand-me-downs or thrift store items. We didn't have much, so I took it upon myself to start working. I'd get to keep half my paycheck, and the other half went to Mom to augment whatever we needed at home.

Working at McDonald's taught me about the importance of systems and hard work. At this early age, I was trained on systems and plugged into an operation that generated millions of dollars. This was incredibly intriguing and eye-opening for me. McDonald's literally had teenagers running this multimillion-dollar business. The power of systems! Systems allow ordinary people to have extraordinary results! I quickly adapted to the systems and climbed the ladder to a managing position before I graduated high school. McDonald's provided an environment where, even though I left smelling of French fry grease, I made noticeable progress, faced challenges, and implemented systems that provided growth.

Once I understood the power of systems, I was able to adapt this same philosophy in my military career. I was the airman revamping systems, creating continuity where there wasn't any, and always looking for better, more efficient ways to do things. One of my zones of genius (or superpowers) is the ability to create systems and find efficient, effective ways to get results with ordinary people. I have adopted systems into many areas of my life, including finding my fighter stance.

It's inevitable! You will get hit. You're in the ring of life; you walk onto the battlefield every morning. You enter the ring knowing that whatever you have planned to do to your opponent, without question, they hold a similar plan. You both have a goal to win and put the other to sleep. As a fighter, you're more likely to be hit because you're out there consistently persisting in pursuit of your greatest potential. You're moving the needle. You're bucking against the status quo. You feel like you're failing. It's guaranteed there will be turbulence.

I'd love to tell you that your days will run smoothly without any bumps, but that is not the case. What I can tell you is this: As a fighter operating at a level most aren't used to, you will have very fulfilling days because you're living out your purpose and potential. But, at the same time, there will be challenges. As a fighter progresses in life, working their way up to a champion title, they will be tested. Are you ready for that next level? Are you willing to put in the work required to reach that level? To be able to get your hands on that title, you'll need to be able to navigate the ring regardless of what battles you find yourself in and what obstacles are thrown your way.

Remember that suffering is necessary to expose a person to their highest self. For a fighter to make the impact they are destined for, to leave a legacy, and to fulfill their potential, this suffering must occur. Adversity is necessary for optimal human development. The challenge must be accepted. Once you fully accept this challenge, without any doubt, you will finally be able to relax and be at ease in the presence of hard work.

You'll understand that problems and challenges arise to bring your attention to a solution, and pain is an indicator that something isn't right and needs to change.

I am here to teach you how to handle these punches, or obstacles, with grace. How to sharpen your weapon and not only defend yourself but also aggressively fight back in the name of purpose. I'm going to teach you how to initiate your fighter stance quickly and defend yourself proactively. My aim is to have you marching off the battlefield minimally damaged, if at all.

FINDING YOUR FIGHTER STANCE

To find your FIGHTer stance when you get hit or a challenge presents itself, you first set the **Foundation.** Then you **Ignite** the fighter within, followed by **GSD** (Get Shit Done, or "get to work") while grasping and understanding our **Heart, Hand,** and **Head** set. Then take **Time** to reflect on lessons learned.

F: FOUNDATION

The first step in initiating your fighter stance is to have a solid foundation. As fighters, our power comes from the ground up: our foundation from the rock on which we stand. What is your foundation made of? The more solid your foundation, the greater your chance of success and triumph in battle. Confidence in your foundation comes from a strong faith and trust in yourself, your identity, and your mission.

Have faith over fear. Understand first and foremost that battles, challenges, punches, and hits strike only to *protect, promote,* or *perfect* us.

Have faith in yourself and your purpose, and know that your mission will prevail. Keep your mind positive. Pray. Remember that you're not alone. The power of purpose is on your side. There is Someone who loves you more than anyone, who wants to see you succeed; recall that Silent Partner we chatted about: your Source, God, the Man with the plan.

Definiteness of purpose is a *must.* Demand the power to prevail. It's important that when you pray or speak to the universe, you do so positively. I understand that the situation may suck. Sucker punches hurt. But you must keep your mind positive. Keep the faith.

"'For I know the plans I have for you,' declares the LORD, 'plans to prosper you and not to harm you, plans to give you hope and a future.'"
–Jeremiah 29:11

When we're trying to progress in life, there will be, without doubt, negative forces wanting us to fail. They want you to get discouraged and depressed, and they most definitely want you to throw in the towel. If you're not the praying type, ask the universe or higher energy to clear the path that your purpose requires. We don't know all the answers, but if we're aligning with our purpose and in action, a solution will be granted and shown to us. But you must be open to listening, being obedient, and taking action even if you don't like the answer.

Remember, action alleviates anxiety, and faith reminds you that you're not alone. Keep your mind in the right place. When we're in the midst of a fight, it's more important than ever that we keep our minds in the game. You will need to constantly be feeding your mind the right "nutrients." Listening to podcasts and audiobooks in congruence with your purpose, reading books and articles in alignment with your truth, plus meditation, prayer, and worship, will all have to be so consistent and exercised around the clock to make sure you stay on track. Stay *focused.*

Generally, the bigger the fight, the more important this step. Grab a book that will boost your attitude. Listen to a motivational message. Stop, drop, and do burpees! Take your mind off what knocked you down and remember the fighter you are. Then, when returning to a state of positivity and reattacking the situation, you will see things clearly. You will be able to problem-solve. You will start to receive the answers and solutions you need to progress.

This is an easy step to forget or put to the side. We talked earlier about the importance of reading and listening to materials that will keep your mind fed with nutrient-dense material and personal development. Don't take this lightly. You may feel the urge to tell yourself, *I am too busy trying to put out this fire right now.* Don't. Amateurs make this mistake. A long time ago, I made this mistake. This step is more important now than ever. During a fire, it's so easy to get distracted by the flame and forget we need to find the tools to put it out. Don't fall into this trap. Feed your mind with the information needed to overcome the obstacle.

Reach out to your mentors. We talked about the power of mentors in the previous chapter. This is another benefit to mentors or masterminds. As entrepreneurs, leaders, change makers, and fighters, we'll get knocked down. It's inevitable. But you'll get back up. How quickly you rise can increase exponentially if you have the right people in your corner to provide perspective and help you problem-solve. It's an incredible feeling to know that you have allies by your side when going to war. Find those mentors.

I: IGNITE

Always choose to fight rather than back down. We always have an option: fight, flight, or freeze. You're a fighter. Wrap up; find that fighter stance. Remember, adversity is required for a human being to reach their true potential. It's time to really focus and say, "Fear, you have no authority here." Make sure your feet are firmly planted on the ground; that foundation is firm, unshakable. Repeat to yourself, "I'll not get knocked down."

A human's natural response is to fall into old patterns or habits. I know this all too well. Understand, failure and defeat are temporary experiences. Self-doubt may kick in, but just like a muscle needs to be conditioned, so does your ability to build confidence.

Confidence is built through competence, which is established through repetition, or reps, or in a figurative sense, punches, kicks, and hits. As you exercise confidence, your self-doubt in situations of failure will decrease. Realize, this too shall pass. Don't quit when you get hit. It's just a hit; you didn't get knocked out.

REMINDER: Everything you need has already been placed in your DNA.

Don't quit on your capability. Don't quit on your potential. Everything you need to get through this battle is already within you. A human's first response is usually to quit, take flight, and run in the opposite direction of adversity. Subjecting yourself to pain is a choice few will make. Not you. You're a fighter. Refuse to throw in the towel. Failure brings a climax in which a fighter has the privilege of clearing their mind of fear and making a new start in a different direction. Look at failure as an opportunity to learn something about yourself. Fear is an emotion that stimulates the body and mind the same way excitement does. Get excited that this pain is an opportunity to grow.

Once you have faced fear and recognized it's only an emotion, it's now time to *identify* the problem, challenge, or threat without involving emotions. Remove personal feelings from the situation. What is the actual problem you're attempting to solve? Do you need to pull back or pivot? What adjustment(s) will you need to make?

Your feelings will lie to you. They'll confuse you about what is really happening. You need to emotionally disconnect and reconnect to the mission. Get out of the room or whatever area you're in for a moment so you can calm down, collect your thoughts, and allow yourself to gain composure so you can clearly identify the issue. This gets easier each time you enter battle because you're learning to respond versus react. You're getting those reps in. Your initial reaction may be to scream, yell, cry, and even quit. Just like a muscle, it takes time to develop a response versus a reaction under tension.

You will get better. Some things need to be corrected on your journey. Most problems and challenges will arise to bring much-needed attention to a possible solution. You can also look at this as a course correction, a detour on your path to potential. You're being asked to change something to promote you to that next level to reach your full potential. Don't ignore this. You'll keep having the same problems until you finally offer a solution. There always is a solution. There is always a lesson to be learned. You're a problem solver and a champion in the making. What is the problem that needs your attention right now?

G: GET TO WORK (Get Shit Done)

As one of my mentors, Bedros Keullian, would say, "Get Shit Done!" A problem or challenge always exists as an indicator that something needs to change. This is an opportunity for you to get better, to level up. This is what you have prepared for, and the tools you need to conquer this opponent, get shit done (GSD), and achieve a victory are already within you.

REMINDER: Get out there and stack some wins.

Our confidence, ego, and heart are usually bruised when we take a hit, depending on the magnitude of the blow. Our minds may not necessarily be able to think in the right direction for the current problem. To find a solution to problems we're facing, we need to be able to operate at our highest level from a place of purpose. To get your groove back, go stack some small wins, even if they don't have to do with the situation.

For example, I'll complete a killer workout. I think best when I am working out, and solutions or action needed will come to me in the middle of an intense workout. Stacking those wins will boost your confidence back up and put you in the right headspace to overcome the sucker punch or hit you just experienced.

Now that you're thinking straight and with purpose, *get to work*. Initiate the Law of GOYA: Get Off Your Ass. Action alleviates anxiety.

Move with intention. Small steps are better than no steps at all. Imperfect progress. Get moving, take action, and you will notice the answers will magically start to appear. Imperfect progress is better than no progress at all, and success loves speed. This is not the time to be a spectator; get your hands in front of your face, initiate that fighter stance, and get in the fight. It's time to start striking back.

If you don't start moving, you'll notice that you find yourself stuck, overthinking, and not taking any action at all. One of my mentors calls this loop "analysis paralysis." You'll be frozen. Don't allow yourself to go there. But if you do find yourself there, recognize it, and then start over at the beginning of this section. Remember you're a fighter. There's nothing wrong with starting over. It's not starting that results in the deepest pain and biggest regret.

H: HAND, HEART, HEAD SET

At the beginning, middle, and for the duration of the fight, it will be important that you continuously take inventory of whether or not the fight you're in falls in line with your values, your purpose, and your priorities. Have you ever found yourself in the middle of a fight you had no business being in? Pleading for a relationship that did not align with your values? Placing minuscule matters in front of your purpose? Letting another's actions dictate your values, causing discomfort and pain, and quite possibly regret? It's very easy to find yourself in battles you don't have any business being in to begin with. To describe this, I love the saying "not my monkeys, not my circus."

Learn to stay in your lane. As a fighter, you may need to quite honestly turn down a fight if it's not your fight to be in. When you allow yourself to get tangled in the chaos and mess of someone else's battle, you'll be ignoring and neglecting your own battles and destiny.

An easy way to tell if you're involving yourself in someone else's battle is to ask yourself these questions:

1. Does it align with my purpose?
2. Are my values being upheld?
3. Is the battle feeding me or bleeding me?

There will be battles you find yourself in that you will know, without question, are not yours. Don't get distracted. Don't let your ego and pride put you up against the ropes, taking hits you have no business taking. You'll be inflicting unnecessary pain on yourself. More importantly, you will be draining the much-needed energy that should be given to bigger and better parts of your world.

T: TIME

Look for the lesson learned. All challenges arise to teach us. You don't fail unless you give up. Learn from this and move forward smarter, stronger, and better prepared for the next hit. As a mentor of mine, David Meltzer, reminds me, "Take time to find the light, the love, and the lesson behind every challenge."

In the military, after any big event or situation, we'd get together as a group to "brain dump." We'd go through the situation and talk about what we could have done better, what could have been done differently or more efficiently, what systems could be created, and what we did well. This is so important. There are many ways to do this; do it however you choose, but get it done.

Some people like to journal. Some just sit and think. You must take time to review and reflect. This will increase your chances of success the next time you encounter a similar situation. I take this one step further every night; I review my day: What went well? What could I have done differently? Did I pursue my potential to the best of my ability?

Additionally, throughout the day, you will hear me say, "That's a win!" Big, small, or anything in between, I do my best to recognize the wins. At night, I'll journal and stack all of the wins throughout the day. This ends my day on a high note and continues to help me look for those wins throughout the next day, to live in a positive flow and an elevated frequency connected to my intention.

The Importance of Self-discipline

This FIGHT system cannot be implemented unless you have the discipline and the desire to become better. A fighter must have resolute discipline as one of their most important core values. It's easy when we get discouraged or sucker punched to quickly fall into old patterns or bad habits. This happens to the best of us.

On March 17, 2020, the COVID pandemic was heating up. I'd been working nonstop for ten weeks straight, 16-hour days. Don't get me wrong, I felt privileged to do so, and I was working in conjunction with my purpose, but frankly, it was exhausting. "Wonderfully exhausting" was usually the response I'd give when someone asked how my day was. I was taking punches left and right, handling them like a fighter, a true boss.

But nonetheless, I was taking hits daily. The economic crash connected to the pandemic had turned my world upside down in the blink of an eye, and I was in the process of rebuilding my business. I was *exhausted*. But I always found the energy to get the necessary work done. It's not coincidental that when you're working in the flow with your purpose, the energy you need to accomplish the mission is effortlessly mustered and administered.

I took a severe hit one day that really hurt. I gasped for breath and wanted to curl up and cry. I wanted to quit. The announcement of a city-wide "shutdown" went from two weeks to four weeks and then to innumerable months! I had no choice but to lay off my team. Unfortunately, no relief was coming from any of my three landlords, and I still had rent and other bills to pay. What would I do?

Failure is a state of mind; therefore, it's something an individual can control until he or she neglects to exercise this privilege. I felt like I had failed. Until I took a step back, took a deep breath, and realized what I was doing.

1. I caught myself wanting to jump back into old patterns and bad habits that didn't serve me.
2. I allowed fear to take control.
3. I did not look for the lesson behind the problem.

As a human being, you're going to fail. You're going to have negative thoughts. You'll mess up. It's okay! You'll never rid yourself of these. However, it's important that when you get stuck in the loop like I did, you can catch yourself, course-correct, and remember your fighter stance. My faith was greater than my fear. I recalled my purpose and continued to work, only this time online. I put together various workout programs that my gym members could do at home. After all, shutdown or no shutdown, they still needed a daily exercise regimen and community support.

When you get hit, implement your FIGHT system:

- **F**OUNDATION of Faith
- **I**GNITE the fighter within
- **G**SD (Get Shit Done, or "Get to work")
- **H**EART, HAND, and HEAD set
- **T**IME to reflect

Create habits that serve you. Your habits will make or break you. New beneficial habits are formed through consistent repetition. The more you do something, the more likely you will continue to do it and build that new habit. Work at it; keep getting those reps in repeatedly until it becomes solid, until the new habit's a part of your lifestyle. Compounded over time, that habit will make the difference between losing and winning the battle.

Systems will help you elevate from ordinary to extraordinary. Systems work regardless of how you're feeling that day. This is the *power* behind implementing systems, but you have to activate them when necessary. The successful, the champions, get to where they are because they can put emotions and feelings aside and get the job done.

ROUND 6 TAKEAWAYS

1. Your fighter stance represents a confident, purpose-driven, fearless fighter. This is your mindset. A fighter's mindset.
2. Remember that suffering is necessary to expose a person to their highest self. For a fighter to make the impact they are destined for, fulfill their potential, and leave a legacy, this suffering is part of the process.
3. As a fighter, your POWER comes from the ground up, and your foundation from the ROCK on which you stand. What is your foundation made of?
4. This FIGHT system cannot be implemented unless you have the discipline and the desire to improve your lot in life.

Round 7

PERFORMING AS A CHAMPION

"The will must be stronger than the skill."
–Muhammad Ali

When you hit that level, that status of "Champion," when you have found your other self: the human you were created to be, and when you start operating in a flow consistent and congruent with intention and purpose… What a feeling!

When you have arrived, you'll know it! Everything seems to operate more smoothly. I'm not saying you're no longer going to get hit. You're in the ring, but this dance you play with your opponent is a bit different now. You "float like a butterfly, sting like a bee." You move like water. You have learned the art of co-creating your life! You're no longer a wandering generality.

You stand tall in confidence, backed by determination and faith in the process and definiteness in your purpose. You're ready to take hits because your fighter stance is locked and dialed in. You're ready for whatever hits are thrown at you. You wake up in the morning with "purpose" as your alarm clock. There is no more hitting the snooze button. When you realize there is purpose and intention to your life, you may no longer need a real alarm clock to wake you up. And you will most nights go to bed… "Wonderfully exhausted!"

"Champions are made from something deep inside them—a desire, a dream, a vision. They have to have the skill, and the will. But the will must be stronger than the skill."
–Mohammad Ali

Every day, as you're walking this path of purpose, you shine. Everything you need to accomplish your purpose finds its way to you. The people, the places, and the materials you need to accomplish your mission show up. Welcome, fighter, to heaven on this side of earth. Declare it now. Feel it now. Embrace it now. The energy you're exuding and your vibration are so high that they repel the mediocre and the status quo. Have faith in the process. This is how champions enter the ring. This is how the successful, the high performers, and the warriors march on this battlefield we call life, on this side of heaven.

Once you hit that status of "Champion," others will flock in your direction and want to know how you did it. People will automatically be drawn to your presence. Those same people who doubted you, mocked you, attempted to bring you down, laughed at you, and told you that you were crazy will want to know how you did it and how you got so lucky.

You'll notice that as you take this path, your circle of friends (or those you thought were friends) starts to shrink. Coincidence? Not at all! Every time you decided to go into battle, fewer allies assisted. That's good; this means you're on the right track. Remember the rule about your associations: you have to guard your circle. Ask yourself again, as you come in contact with more people: *Do they align with my purpose and values?* This concept was hard for me to accept. I'm the type who wants to save them all. Carry everyone on my back through the battlefield. I'll dash back into the battle, attempting to save everyone.

Understand this: Not everyone can be saved. Not everyone *wants* to be saved. You cannot save someone who does not want to be saved. And you certainly cannot build with someone who doesn't want to help you carry the bricks. You can't throw someone else's punches.

Opportunity falls empty on people without drive and determination. You can literally show them the Yellow Brick Road to success, but they will be blinded by an aversion to hard work, and they're big on excuses. They are where they are in their journey, and that is okay. Remember, you were once there too; have grace and choose to move forward. Choose carefully whom you align with; you want allies, not adversaries. Remember this truth: Everything and everyone you need to succeed will be given to you as long as you're in alignment with your calling and purpose.

Be careful. Be diligent. As a champion, you will continue to be tested to reach that next level and live out your purpose. Remember: Champions are always in consistent pursuit of their potential (also known as "living with intention"). Don't get distracted. Don't lose your focus. Keep your eyes on the prize. Never forget: You're a champion!

Reaching the status of "Champion" of power, influence, and leadership requires consistent upkeep and responsibility. The same disciplines that helped you achieve that status must be maintained and upgraded, or you will feel your title start to slip away. That is the incredible feeling of flow, operating as your "other self," or as I like to say, "operating from spirit, not from your flesh, and working in your purpose in congruence with your Source or the Universe." This can be stripped away quickly if you're not careful. If you're not diligent, you'll drift off course. You'll lose a round. Then the next, and the next, etc. Your title is always on the line. I am not here to tell you about rainbows and waterfalls and this beautiful paradise you'll be in once you hit champion status. I am here as your coach to KEEP. IT. REAL. The truth is, your title is always on the line. The truth is, it's not easy. The truth is, if you *don't* get up every day and "carry your cross" to answer the calling on your life to "Get Shit Done," you'll quickly fall back into spectator status.

When you do lose your focus, and sometimes you will, make sure you do all that you can to get back in that state of flow. You must be prepared to initiate "Operation: Course Correct." What'll happen is you'll get so comfortable in this state of flow that the habits that created this state will be forgotten. You will simply stop doing them. It could start with hitting the snooze button when you wake up. Or missing the 10 pages of reading for the day. You may even skip a workout or two. We do this because we're humans who operate in an imperfect world. But you must be able to catch yourself before it gets out of hand. You must become a champion at consistently applying discipline to master the mundane.

Just like discipline, *focus* is a muscle that must be exercised daily. It's easy in this world of quick fixes, silver bullets, and "the next best thing" to get off track. When you start finding success and operating at champion status, others will take note of the strategies, disciplines, habits, and tactics that have earned you that title. Many people will start competing or asking for your time, advice, help, and resources.

New opportunities will come your way, plus new adventures and relationships. I am not saying to ignore these; instead, analyze the new options or opportunities, then ask yourself, *Does this align with my purpose and mission?* If so, move forward. However, the same opportunities and relationships will also cross your path, easily distracting you and throwing you off course.

Champions can and will lose their titles. It's happened many times. I'm sure you're aware of situations where individuals let ego, fame, and glory overtake their purpose. Don't let that be you. Don't become one of the distressing statistics.

But if it does happen, and it probably will, you can reclaim your title. Reclaim your champion status.

It has happened to me a few times, where either doubt, fear, exhaustion, glory, or pure laziness has taken my title from me. When I say "taken from me," you feel it. There is a distinct difference between operating in a state of flow aligned with your purpose, mission, and values versus not. When you're operating at a champion level, everything seems to come naturally. You're operating in a state of ease. Like, you want to pinch yourself and ask, "Am I dreaming?" The people and the opportunities all seem to "magically" align.

Until they don't.

When this disconnect happens, ask yourself this: *Am I adhering to the same disciplines that brought me to this point?* Chances are unlikely. I'm repeating this because it's so important: You were so busy and distracted by your champion status that you didn't read your ten pages of a book that day. You skipped a workout because *What is one workout when I've done so many, and today I'm tired?* The excuses start to override the reasons you were applying those disciplines. The "magic" was in the *consistency*.

When I have been thrown off course and start taking increased damage, the trials and challenges seem to be overflowing. Or when battles become increasingly difficult, and I start to doubt my abilities and my mission, this is a sign to stop and inventory my Five Pillars: spiritual, physical, mental, professional, and relationships. I've noticed that if I'm not consistently pursuing my potential in these five areas and not performing in congruence with my values and intention, my life will seem "off balance."

Now, let me take a moment to address a question I am often asked: "How do you find balance?" I don't believe that you can achieve perfect balance in life. Any entrepreneur or champion who's successful and consistently in pursuit of that next level will tell you there's no such thing as perfect balance. When we choose to say yes to one decision, we're ultimately saying no to another. There is a sacrifice somewhere to someone or something. There's such a deep investment in self and your potential that the world will start to give you remarks, such as "You're obsessed," "You're selfish," or "You work too much." Your environment will look and feel dramatically different than that of your peers. When you start to live with intention, the only balance you'll find is that of being in conscious congruency with who you're created to be.

On the other hand, when you're not in sync with your values, mission, and intention, this is where you'll find that you feel off balance, especially when you have had a taste of, or have experienced, champion status.

You can achieve a sense of completeness and satisfaction every day by consistently pursuing your potential and actively working toward your purpose. However, during this champion process, you'll inevitably get thrown off course. When this happens, when you feel out of flow, inventory the following five areas immediately. And let's be real, it was because you stopped inventorying these areas that you were thrown off course to begin with. That's okay, you're human, but we *must* course-correct right away.

1. Spiritual: Am I in consistent connection with my Higher Power or the energy from the universe that supports me? It's easy to ask for help or guidance when things are going wrong or not in our favor. When things start going well, when we're in that flow state, we can quickly lose sight of the forces that brought us to that state, no longer tapping into them daily. It's important that you continue to pray and/or meditate and connect with the positive energy that is available to you. We can easily disconnect from this higher source and fall into old, unsupportive patterns, behaviors, and habits. We start to go back to old thinking or believe that we can do this alone. What happens next is that we try to start fighting battles alone. We get tired and weary. We want to quit the game.

As an amateur fighter, I'd allow myself to stay in this state far too long. I'd wallow in my failures or dread getting up. I'd start to identify with a victim mentality. I'd fall back into those old behavior patterns. I'd take for granted the Senior Partner I have access to. Wayne Dyer points out in *The Power of Intention* that this Senior Partner has never abandoned me and has stuck with me, even in moments when I had seemingly deserted my Source. This infinite Source, God, is at your fingertips. You did not get to where you are without it, so why do you think you can continue to grow without consistent communication? There is a Source available for you to use, to grow to significant proportions, and to accomplish your missions. Don't forget that. Ask for help daily and declare your intentions.

2. Physical: Throughout this book, I have mentioned many of the systems, techniques, and mental exercises I use and related them to our body's muscles. The human body is made to move. The adage says, "If you don't use it, you'll lose it." A healthy body contributes to a healthy mind and heart. You cannot perform at your peak mentally without taking care of your body. I am not talking about diets and fads; rather, a lifestyle that incorporates consistent exercise daily. With a background in fitness, I obviously advocate exercise daily. Studies show that you should get at least thirty minutes of exercise each day.

When life gets busy, we'll forgo a workout or healthy meal options because we don't have time. However, you must continue to make exercise and a healthy diet a priority in your daily routine. Intentionally putting your body under tension through exercise and then fueling properly and consistently is mandatory if you want to continually perform as a champion.

A healthy diet is a must. Our minds and bodies won't function at an optimal level if we're feeding ourselves trash. Food is fuel. You're not some beater vehicle. Imagine your dream car: ______________________ (insert it here). What type of fuel and maintenance is required? You're not a low-grade vehicle, so don't treat yourself like one.

After exercise and nutrition, sleep is a must. "I'll sleep when I am dead" is a bunch of crock! Your body needs consistent rest. I recommend

6-8 hours a day. Everyone is different, but find where you work at max capacity and productivity based on your sleep level. Some need more than others. Additionally, too much sleep is also harmful. Stick to a routine, the same bedtime and wake-up time, even on weekends. Remember, the magic is found in *consistency*.

3. Mental: What are you thinking? Literally, what types of thoughts are you having throughout the day? We have hit on this in previous chapters about the importance of what you allow into your head. It's so important that your head is right mentally. This starts with your beliefs; learn to question them. Are they serving you? Your beliefs will lead to your thoughts, and your thoughts to your actions. Your actions produce your results.

Every morning, I start with a motivational video or a reading. There's so much garbage out there that you need to intentionally feed yourself positive thoughts. Again, this is a must to perform at the top levels. Negative thoughts are like weeds; they will find a way to creep in. You must make a point to notice when this happens and have a way to terminate the detrimental thoughts.

Some of the habits I've incorporated into my day include listening to a morning motivational speech. There are hundreds of them on YouTube or podcasts. I usually keep it short, about fifteen minutes or less, sometimes while I get my workout in or during my cardio. Whenever I am driving, I have a podcast playing to fill my subconscious with uplifting messages and beliefs. Then there's uplifting music. I listen to praise and worship music to instantly remind me that I am not alone.

4. Professional: As busy professionals, we can sometimes get stuck. As champions, we need to continuously be challenged to feel fulfilled. When you find yourself bored at work or lacking passion, it's time to change it up. If you cannot find joy in what you're doing, pay someone to do it or find something else to do. As a champion, you need to continue to advance your skills, invest in yourself, and create. Your potential is infinite, which means you always need to be growing and developing your skills and talents.

I have noticed more recently that when you're operating at champion status, life will throw you into a state of discomfort. This discomfort can come in the form of pain, trial, challenge, or tribulation. This is God's way of getting you to level up or ascend into who you were created to be.

In 2020, we were in the throes of the COVID-19 pandemic. I was presented with the choice to either level up or fall down and fail. I say "choice" and not "forced" because it was definitely a choice. There have been handfuls of businesses that continue to drop off the map because they refused to level up or just downright gave up. God wants us content, not complacent. He cares far more about your character than your comfort. Embrace the discomfort; learn to expect it. Have a mindset shift from "Why is this happening *to* me?" to "This is happening *for* me!"

Champions don't give up. We pivot, we problem solve, we find solutions, we adapt, we fight back, we overcome, and we conquer. We continue to increase our skill set. We take self-improvement courses. We seek out individuals who have the knowledge and experience to help us get where we want to be.

The person you are today isn't the person you need to be to advance to that next level or continue your mission and purpose. Continued education is a must to develop into the person, the fighter, and the champion you need to be to live out your purpose.

Remember, as fighters and as champions, we're in consistent pursuit of our potential. I continuously take courses in business, exercise, science, spirituality, and personal development. Plus, I attend seminars and workshops that focus on what I am passionate about pursuing. Likewise, on occasion, I dabble in things outside of my norm to challenge myself further, to push my limits, and to get me out of my comfort zone. This keeps the brain fresh and continuously firing.

Are you continually looking for ways to advance your purpose? Are you performing at your potential? When was the last time you did something to increase your knowledge and skill set? What can you do today to go from hitting the status quo to being great?

5. Relationships: This is a big one: Who are the people you associate with most? What does your inner circle look like? What about your outer circle? Who are you surrounded by and influenced by? I was once a people pleaser. I'd constantly seek approval from others. Additionally, I allowed other people's actions, opinions, and behaviors to influence mine. I want you to notice what I said there. Let me repeat it: I *allowed* it. Understand that as a fighter, you're responsible for yourself. Your actions, your associations, and your thoughts are under your control.

We discussed this in a previous chapter, but it's so important that it's worth repeating: the quickest way to get thrown off track is to hang around individuals who hold much lesser values than you do. You can start to mimic their habits and behaviors. It includes family and significant others. Are your relationships in good standing? Do you need to start limiting the time you spend with certain people who are not at your level? Do you need to start communicating differently with a significant other in an effort to put your relationship in a positive light?

You attract individuals into your life who are in parallel with the vibration and energy you release. Who are you attracting? What energy are you putting into the universe to attract these people? Take a moment and inventory those around you. Have you allowed some "energy vampires" to sneak into your circle? Have you let old patterns and behaviors put you back in situations that don't serve you? Are you the smartest, most experienced, and most successful person in your circle, and no one else can come close to keeping up with you?

This is *so* important. You have to stop right now. Be honest with yourself. Drop the ego. Then ask yourself, *Who do I need to release from my inner circle? And who do I need to seek out to be the best version of me and become the champion I am meant to be?*

Also, ask yourself, *Am I giving my attention and intention to these five areas of my life: spiritual, physical, mental, professional, and relational?*

Where your attention and intention collide, you will inevitably see coincidences appear, or what others may call "luck." It's those small disciplines compounded over time that produce lucky coincidences, massive results, and huge success. Contrarily, if we fail to uphold the same disciplines, life will seem less purposeful because we soon become aware that we're not living life to our fullest potential.

It's important that you regularly inventory these five areas. Self-reflection and evaluation are great tools for success. Take the time to reflect and review, which takes us right back to the "T" for "Time" in our FIGHTer stance. Right when you notice that emptiness, that lack of your purpose, review the five areas. Where have you been lacking? What can you change?

Evaluate yourself: Give yourself a grade on a scale of 1-10, where 1 signifies that you feel you have no purpose, and 10 represents you're in flow and operating in alliance with your purpose. Can you say you have honestly been pursuing your potential in those five areas? Be honest with yourself. Pain is a great indicator that something needs to change. If you're feeling off, discouraged, stressed, depressed, or drained, go through the list. Without question, you'll discover that you're lacking in one or more of those five areas. Identify what is missing. Identify the disciplines you let fall to the wayside, and then get to work on reclaiming them.

A champion knows exactly what it feels like to be performing as one. When you finally grab hold of that title, it comes with a responsibility to continue to work for it, to hold onto it. The work doesn't stop; in fact, it has just begun. Let's fight, and let's win, my champions!

ROUND 7 TAKEAWAYS

Are you regularly taking the time to inventory the five pillars? Do that now. Rate yourself on a scale of 1-10 in each of the five areas, where "1" represents a complete and utter lack of balance, and "10" represents a sense of flow state and completeness in that area.

- Spiritually:
- Mentally:
- Professionally:
- Physically
- Relationships:

For any areas listed above where you scored a "7" or below, revisit that section in this chapter to determine at least one action you can immediately take to increase your score and operate as a champion in all five pillars.

Round 8

STACKING YOUR WINS

"When your desires are strong enough you will appear to possess superhuman powers to achieve them."
–Napoleon Hill

Panting for air, my muscles were depleted, and sweat was dripping down my face; I'd finally reached the top of the mountain. I jumped up on a bench that was perfectly positioned so I could look over Colorado Springs. Raising my hands in the air, I looked to the clouds, and tears filled my eyes.

"Melissa, it was just a hike. Why are you so emotional?" you may ask. It's twofold, really. One, I am an emotional person to start with. Two, I had just pushed myself beyond my comfort zone. Bedros Keuilian, a mentor and author of *Man Up,* taught me that you do tough things on the weekends, so when you face challenges during the week, they don't seem so difficult. Success leaves clues. I implemented his advice, and that's why I had tears.

Let me further explain. For my Saturday workout, I started with a resistance-training leg workout composed of supersets and walked out of the gym feeling like my legs were Jell-O. On Sunday, I did a kickboxing workout. This was to accomplish what I call my "100 Challenge," completing 100 kicks for each leg in a variety of styles, with jump roping and speed bag work between sets. This was difficult after a heavy leg workout the day prior. However, total soreness had not set in yet, but I could feel the fatigue. It takes self-discipline to continue through and not settle for anything short of maximum output. In my head, I heard Ed Mylett, mentor and author of *The Power of One More,* commanding, "Max it out! One more rep!" Once I finished this workout, I headed directly to the aforementioned mountain for hill sprints.

Not a casual stroll in the mountains, but a hard-driving uphill sprint. I felt my legs burning with each stride. I began to question myself through this discomfort. Quitting enters my thoughts. Slowing down becomes an option. It's uncomfortable, it sucks, and it hurts!

I knew that once I reached the mountaintop, I could reclaim my champion status. Neither quitting nor slowing down was an option. Instead, I always choose to push forward, despite the discomfort.

I earned that title, and the view from the top was breathtaking. At this pinnacle, I could see from Colorado Springs all the way to Kansas, with the mountains behind me: Pikes Peak to the south of Colorado Springs. The clouds felt like they were within reach. It was a special feeling when I had pushed myself past the status quo and mediocrity. The view was so much different because I hadn't just gone the extra mile; rather, the distance past the extra mile was "empty." The views were brighter. The winning is different at this level: You grasp destiny firm in your grip and armor yourself for the next climb.

I reflected on my week as I ascended the mountain that day, on the challenges and the wins. It was a tough week, but I reminded myself of my mission and vision. The challenging moments came with lessons, and the lessons with progress. I was one step closer to fulfilling my destiny.

To continuously perform as a champion, you'll need to consistently force yourself out of your comfort zone, or you will not grow, nor will you level up. You must consistently pursue your "fighter" potential. When I hit the top of the mountain, the tears were those of gratefulness. I intentionally forced myself out of my comfort zone to grow and increase my fighter IQ.

A fighter consistently trains. A fighter stays prepared. She or he is always conditioned for that next fight. I get it. I feel pure joy in my pain when I am progressing. This is what humans are meant to do. We're designed to grow through the pain, but it ultimately boils down to making the choice to grow versus remaining average.

What happens when you get to the top of the mountain? What's next? Stop, breathe, and take in the view. Relish in the lessons learned and stack those wins.

With my eyes full of tears, it hit me: You don't stay at the top of the mountain. You're not done. You may have completed a mission. You may have won a round. But you still have a purpose. There is still work to be done.

Watch out for false summits. Amid a victory, hands raised high, you will get hit to the gut. Usually followed by an "Oh shit!" Because you have arrived at a false summit. You thought you made it to the top, but you didn't take time to reflect or continue to follow the process. Your vision became blurry, and you fell back into old patterns and habits. This is an amateur's mistake.

Take time to reflect and really learn the lesson this time, and yes, you guessed it: gear up and start climbing that next mountain. You must get back to work and prove that you've learned your lesson. You head back down to the bottom, where you take what you've learned and apply it to new challenges and come out more successful with less tension than last time.

Also, grab a few allies on the way. It's your responsibility as a leader and a champion, as someone who has been in the trenches, to not only build allies but also help others scale similar mountains and win more fighting rounds in their lives. The time you spent in the ring has taught you valuable lessons. There have been mentors, guides, coaches, and allies on your journey.

This is how we "pay rent" for being on this earth. It's our duty and obligation to serve others. Be an open book and help others with similar dreams, desires, and determination to do what you have done. This will come to be one of the most rewarding parts of your journey. It's your turn to look down from that mountain and help someone else scale it. It's your turn to be in someone's corner and "wrap their hands." You'll become that flashlight that helps direct their path down that dark tunnel. The wisdom you've attained is now going to be poured into others.

Most people focus solely on the destination. The big win. The title fight. Your purpose every day is to chase your destiny unequivocally, inexcusably, and faithfully with passion. You must refuse to surrender until you're dead. The destination for a fighter, for the champion reading this book, comes from an eternal perspective. It's about the journey.

Your ultimate destination is no longer a given point; rather, it's a continuous journey to get up every day and pursue your next best version of yourself. And, because you and I don't know what our best self is, we leave it to "the Man with the plan." We just vow to get up every day and get after it. I promise, your "best self" and your ultimate destination are far better than you can ever imagine or dream of. You achieve them by refusing to quit and staying in the game, no matter the obstacles.

Get ready to scale your next mountain and level up again; you're not done yet. But this time, you're stronger, and with a better understanding that with each summit, with each victory, comes the unlocking of a better, stronger champion. It's time to get back in the ring and continue to put in the work.

As a champion, you don't just climb mountains; you attack every mountain with intention and purpose. You know you will get hit along the way; you may even be taken off course. But because you have tools and techniques in your arsenal, you're now prepared for adversity. Remember, it's not a matter of *if*, but *when* adversity hits.

As a pro fighter, mountains no longer intimidate you. Not for long anyway. You raise your hands in the air and appreciate the work needed to get you to the top. You're consistently looking for other peaks to summit. You're challenging yourself daily to make yourself better.

Embrace The Suck

But wait. There is something I need you to understand. I am talking to you, Champion. Without question, if you're reading this book, and you have made it this far, whether it was out of pure curiosity or because you knew there was something missing, there is something you need to understand: You need to *embrace the suck factor.* There is a suck factor in being a fighter, a high performer, and an intention-driven individual. In part, taking residence in that top tier of five to ten percenters, you'll inevitably have seasons in your life that suck. The reason you're in that top tier is that you're able to embrace it.

Suck, pain, discomfort. Grinding away for hours, days, weeks, and what may seem never-ending at times. As a fighter, you're constantly in the trenches, coming up with new ways to make this world better. That's shit superheroes do, not the average human who has settled for the status quo.

When you hit those suck moments, when you're exhausted, remember that this is part of the process. When life hits you with a sucker punch, be thankful. This is an opportunity for you to rise out of your comfort zone and grow. Hear this: Say it out loud, "I embrace this challenge! This is what I have been preparing for, and I am ready! Throw it at me! I'll attack this hill, and I'll overcome this challenge! I am a fighter! Is this all you've got?"

You're going to hit high moments; those are easy to be thankful for and to celebrate. But the winners, the champions, celebrate the low moments too, because this is where we grow, learn lessons, and find humility.

It's All About Perspective

I have competed in fitness competitions for years. Initially, I chose to participate in them in an effort to combat all of the labels and negative energy from past relationships that did not serve me. I was in pursuit of regaining my self-worth. When I began to recoup my self-worth, remove labels, and change my belief system, this journey proved to be so much more.

The process to prep for one of these competitions is intense, to say the least. It requires a huge amount of self-discipline, dedication, and learning to embrace the suck. The major "suck factor" comes at about six weeks out from a competition. You begin to eliminate many of the extras from your diet. As you get closer to the big show date, week by week, more and more is eliminated. Sugars, fats, carbs, sodium, and those cheat meals that you used to look forward to all start to float away in the sea of "not necessary."

It took me a few shows over multiple seasons to start to clearly see the lesson I needed to learn through this process. As I entered this "suck factor" of competition prep, I'd focus on what I couldn't have (i.e., the sugars, alcohol, fats, carbs, sodium, cheat meals) instead of focusing on what I *could* have.

You see, when you can shift your mind in a "suck factor" situation, your world will evolve. Reframe the situation and try this: instead of…

I can't	□ I can
Why me?	□ Try Me
Set back	□ Set up
I have to	□I get to
What if	□ Even if

Add some of your own here:

1. ____

2. ____

3. ____

Learning to shift your mental state as a champion and to reframe "the suck" is vital in battle. This is a habit that needs to be built and practiced consciously until it's wired into your subconscious. It's inevitable that you will come across situations that are not ideal, which challenge you and make you question your destiny. This is normal, but the quicker you can reframe the situation and understand that every challenge is an opportunity to learn a lesson, the less you will struggle. When you come across one of these situations, quickly activate your fighter stance and get to work. You have a title to uphold and claim. Everything is already within you. Choose to use this setback as a setup. These "why me" challenges quickly turn into "try me" wins.

Celebrating Wins

When you're operating as a champion, you're in consistent pursuit of that next level. The next challenge. The next opportunity. This means you're making progress because you're entering the ring of life and fighting. This is where champions belong. These fights you enter consist of rounds or chapters. You'll get hit, you'll get knocked out, and you'll get sucker punched. You'll also give hits, win rounds, and retain your title. It happens. It's all part of your journey.

Stack those wins. That's what we do! Champions thrive on accomplishment, change, and impact. During this process, it's necessary to notice the small wins and celebrate them. When you wake up early in the morning, and you don't hit the dreaded snooze button, WIN! When you make that bed first thing, WIN! Did you accomplish your workout first thing? WIN! Stack the wins! Accomplish your GSD (Get Shit Done) list? WIN! When you start racking up wins and *noticing* them, large or small, the energy you're creating forces you to continue to look for wins and build momentum for the day and for your *next* win.

Celebrating The Losses

Celebrating the wins is easy! Learning to celebrate the losses is a bit more of a challenge. But you get to. Regardless of the outcome, if you're passionately chasing your destiny unequivocally, inexcusably, and faithfully, be proud! If it was a loss, or you feel like you failed, reframe it.

As David Meltzer explains so well in *Connected to Goodness*, look for the light, the love, and the lesson in the situation. Be accountable. How did you participate in this outcome? What did you do well? What could you have done differently?

When you slip, especially when it comes to building a new habit like not hitting the snooze button, take accountability for the situation. Acknowledge it, then commit to making it happen the next day. It does not do you any good to spend time stressing over a missed opportunity or a mess-up. It's wasted energy. Learn from it, acknowledge it, and commit to doing better; then move the fuck on! Keep your mind in a consistent state of moving forward.

Celebrate you! Be in love with your life, every minute of it. You need to understand that even with a bad economy or negative people, your slip-ups don't change your mission. They don't change your DNA. Remember who you are, and learn to tell your hurt feelings to take a hike!

Operating At Your Peak

You have a mission and a purpose to fulfill that can only be accomplished by you. It would be selfish to stop. You were made for this. To perform as a fighter, you need to make sure to take care of yourself. Throughout this journey, you will need to prioritize yourself. You cannot serve at your fullest if you're not operating at your fullest.

Fighters, overachievers, go-getters, and winners inevitably will push themselves into the ground before quitting. To the point where they are close to being unable to make their next move. When in constant movement forward toward our mission and purpose, we do whatever it takes to get the job done, yes! But at the same time, this can be detrimental to you and your purpose if you're not careful.

What do I mean by that? You're not able to take care of others if you don't take care of yourself first. You work hard mentally, physically, and emotionally. You operate at what you hope to be 100 percent effort, 100 percent of the time. When a champion is passionately chasing their intention faithfully and squashing excuses as they arise, it is difficult to find the "off" switch. There's no such thing as "off." You're always "on" because it's in your DNA to live your purpose, to be in that flow.

This is normal. When you find the love and the joy in everything you do, why would you want to turn that off or take a break from it? Funny thing, I actually had someone feel sorry for me because my days were so long. I remember staring at him, confused. It baffled me when he said with gloom, "Wow, that's a long day."

Granted, for the average low achiever, fourteen- to sixteen-hour days may seem long, especially if you're doing something you don't particularly like or enjoy. I said right back to him, "There isn't anything else I'd rather be doing."

He tilted his head. "That's unfortunate," said the man, who I knew was content working for minimum wage.

That's average thinking, status mediocre, status quo. Average humans, or those just drifting through life, will have a difficult time understanding the language of a champion because we refuse to operate at that level or low vibration.

I find so much happiness and receive so much joy in what I get to do every day. This did not happen by accident. As you start to apply the tools, techniques, and principles outlined in the previous chapters, you'll notice that it does not matter what you're doing, for how long you're doing it, or where you're at when everything you're doing comes from a place of gratitude and love. Your energy is higher. Your heart is open and ready to give and to receive. You're working in harmony with your Creator.

The fighter name or nickname I've had for years is "The Machine," given to me by my fitness bootcamp clients as a reference to my inability to shut off and my ability to just keep going, no matter the task, challenge, or amount of time required. I'd always be "on" despite what may be happening in my life or any excuse I could possibly come up with; you'd never know, because I just *go*. When I am in service to others, the level of energy I have just seems to increase exponentially. This also holds true in my personal world with my kids. There is no excuse valid enough to make me stop. This is probably why I find it difficult to understand others who make excuses for their inadequacies. My mantra has always been "Find a way." (Just like with Mom, it'd be a rare occasion if I ever saw her surrender to a circumstance or an excuse.)

When you have no other option but to persist, because there is no "Plan B," you'll always problem-solve, come up with solutions, and find a way. If there isn't a door opening for you, you create a door to open.

This alter ego I live by, "The Machine," knows no limits. She understands and produces grade A work, excitement, and joy when in the presence of those she serves. Rarely will she complain or show up at anything below 100 percent. (Although I do have the occasional slip-up; we all do; we're human. Give yourself grace and, you guessed it, move on.) There is no other option.

Operating at this level takes a certain type of understanding and preparation. Yes, preparation. Everything I've discussed in previous chapters, from filling your cup with the right associations, the things you're listening to and reading, and your workouts, all matter when feeding this alter ego, this champion-level work.

A daily habit and practice that has kept me performing at my best is one I often refer to as "disconnecting to reconnect." Sometimes I'd find myself getting irritated, lacking creativity, or not having the ability to solve simple challenges that came up. I wouldn't be able to focus. I would lose drive and motivation. There were even times I wanted to hit the dreaded snooze button on my alarm clock and sacrifice my goals for a few moments of mediocre sleep. I'd then end up discouraged the rest of the day because I started off on the wrong foot.

How did I end up in this state of uneasiness? I did not take proper care of myself. To be able to operate at their peak, a fighter must recover, refuel, and recharge emotionally, spiritually, and physically. Being able to recover, refuel, and recharge is just as important as the mission. In fact, they coexist: you cannot operate at your peak unless you're refilling your tank. Your mission and purpose will be impacted negatively if you're not able to access all your tools and resources properly.

Champions operate so differently from the masses. Our work at times may seem daunting, overwhelming, and never-ending. We may start to question our abilities, strengths, and talents. When you have a purpose connected to a greater Source, obstacles will be put in your way to take you off your path.

If your mission and purpose impact positivity, the greater good, and serving, then everything that comes from you needs to be with intent, conviction, and full of hope. But where do you draw from?

It was not until I realized I needed to *disconnect to reconnect* that I fully understood the importance of refilling my cup, not just daily, but often throughout the day. My morning routine is the most important part of my day. It sets the tone and foundation for the rest of the day. From 3:30 to 6:30 a.m., those three hours are the most important to me. They have become so ingrained in who I have become that I can't imagine starting my day any other way.

My precious three hours, uninterrupted in almost complete silence, are where it's quiet enough to hear my thoughts. I pop out of bed most days stoked at the opportunity to be me. My alarm goes off, but most days I'll wake up about five minutes before it. In those five minutes lying there, I remind myself that I am grateful to be awake and breathing, because some people did not wake up today.

I lay in gratitude, listing all that I am grateful for: waking up breathing, the bed that I am in, and the roof over my head; the list goes on and on. My mind then shifts to visualizing my day. This is not too difficult, as I set the tone for today the night before. I know what I'll conquer today and the impact I'll have. But it starts with gratitude for the opportunity to even wake up and chase after that best version of me, knowing that my day is ready for what I, and only I, can contribute to it.

We're created with an intention specific to us and an opportunity to live that intention every day, but it does require that you activate it daily. That you feel it, believe it, and chase after it. As some might say, we get up every day and "carry our cross."

Another daily habit I use to continue to operate at my peak is meditation. Now, I'm not talking about a yoga pose, hands pressed together in meditation. For all of you who do that, if it works for you, keep doing it. My meditation takes place on the mountain or through some sort of physical exertion. When I am physically pushing myself to my limits, it releases a sense of power and reminds me who I am and *who* is in my corner.

This can happen any time. Today, for example, my day started strong, as most of my days do. I got out of bed. I was stacking wins. I got up without hitting the snooze button, drank my water, and read a few pages of a personal development book to get my mind moving. I jumped in my car and cranked up the Christian rock station, my favorite part of my morning. As I drove to the gym, the music reminded me of my purpose. I sang, I prayed, and I walked into my workout grateful to have arrived and excited for the opportunity to make an impact today. I crushed my workout.

This is just another opportunity for me to level up and prep for the day, reminding myself that I am in control of my thoughts and behavior. After setting myself up for success, like I do every morning, it happens. I get confronted with challenges. This day, it was challenge after challenge. I seemed to hit a negative part of the world multiple times in a matter of hours.

It becomes daunting. When you work so hard to make sure your day is set up for success, your mind is set to "positive." It's inevitable that you will run into negative people, situations, and circumstances. Trouble is unavoidable. Why? Because you can't control everything. But what you can control is how you respond.

I handled the situations with grace. I looked for the light, the love, and the lessons, as my mentor, David Meltzer, has instructed me to do. But I must admit it took a lot out of me. And this was not the first time something like this has happened. So, I knew what I needed.

You see, this is what sets winners apart from losers and champions apart from the mediocre. Most would dwell in the negativity of the day and just produce mediocre results, if any.

But not us, not fighters, not you, the Champion.

I knew what I needed to do. I needed to realign. I needed to remove myself from the world and come back to a place of peace. I needed to go to a place where I controlled my environment. I needed to tap out… temporarily. I needed to freeze, not fight. Freeze, not flee. I needed to get in realignment with my best self and operate from there, not from my emotions. I headed to the mountaintop. My AirPods in, podcast playing, I attacked the hills.

REMINDER: Temporary tap-outs may be necessary for maximum productivity.

As champions, we don't walk up hills; we attack them! I pushed myself to the point of tears, sometimes cursing at the situations that hit me, sometimes in complete silence. After I got to the top, I took a moment to breathe. I looked down and smiled. I raised my hands to the sky and let the sun hit my face. This overwhelming feeling of gratitude washed over me. I thanked the universe for the opportunities I've been given and the challenges I must conquer. I asked for strength, guidance, and the discipline to overcome. I stated my purpose out loud multiple times.

My purpose: to live my life (mind, body, soul, and spirit) with unequivocal intention. Write your purpose here:

____

____

The act of writing and *reciting* your purpose is so powerful! Do it often. Place it on sticky notes or notecards. Place them where you can see them and read them often. (When asked what you do for a living, you'll be ready to deliver your **purpose**.)

I acknowledge my mission and then ask again for the strength, guidance, wisdom, and discipline to accomplish it. I then remember who *I am.*

Remember that you're a child of the Most High God: Yahweh. You're powerful beyond measure, living in an abundant universe. Your purpose and mission will launch you into action. Backed up by faith, I'm reminded that I am capable of whatever I set my mind to and whatever I'm willing to act on. Remember, whatever you give attention and intention to will create the coincidences or luck in your universe.

It's without question that you'll have days when you're caught off guard, when there are negative and toxic people in your path. Where sucker punches collide with your plans. When you feel like quitting, operating as a champion at an optimal level requires understanding that you're going to have challenges, but you have tools and techniques in place to keep you operating at optimal levels. It's not about how many times you get knocked down; it's about how many times you get back up. Now, get back up and fight.

The quote at the beginning of this chapter by Napoleon Hill comes to life when you tap into your purpose consistently and align yourself with your Source. Steadily performing as a champion requires continuous interaction and connection with the Source you have in your corner. Activating and staying in congruence with your purpose, you will appear to possess superhuman powers to the outside world and those around you. Accept the power and use it to create.

ROUND 8 TAKEAWAYS

1. Your ultimate destination is no longer a given point; rather, it's a continuous accomplishment to get up every day and pursue your next best version of yourself.

2. To perform as a champion, you will need to consistently force yourself out of your comfort zone; otherwise, you will not grow, and you will not level up. You must pursue your "fighter" potential.

3. You must disconnect to reconnect. Being able to recover, refuel, and recharge is just as important as your mission. In fact, they coexist. You cannot operate at your peak unless you're filling your tank.

4. It's our duty and obligation to serve others. Be an open book and help others with similar dreams, desires, and determination to do what you have done. This will come to be one of the most rewarding parts of your journey here on earth.

Round 9

JUST WHEN YOU THINK YOU HAVE WON

"The ultimate measure of a man is not where he stands in moments of comfort and convenience, but where he stands at times of challenge and controversy."
–Martin Luther King Jr.

Hold that belt high! Arms raised in the air, you're the champion! Success surrounds you. You're at the top of the mountain. The fight is finally over. The blood, sweat, and tears were all worth it! You have this overwhelming feeling of happiness and fulfillment. You look down from the mountaintop to see the world around you. You have accomplished your mission, your goal, your dream. What you set out to do, you have done it.

But then, just like that… it could be a moment later, maybe even a day or perhaps a week after that high of accomplishing the task you set out to complete, when you may suddenly feel empty.

What does success look like to you? To me, it was finding that one special person and living happily ever after. Success to me was being able to provide *more* for my kids than my mom did for my siblings and me. Success to me was the bigger house with all the fine furnishings and a fridge that was always full. My definition of success continued to evolve as I matured. Success, I thought, was having my own gym, where I made the rules and was in charge of my time and money freedom. Success was having extra money at the end of the month and not living paycheck to paycheck. Success to me was not having to rely on anyone but myself, not a government handout, not a man coming to my rescue.

All those items I so eloquently cut out of magazines for my very first vision board and every vision board after that. I started either acquiring or accomplishing, which brought temporary happiness and pleasure. Certifications, job positions, milestones, competitions, income levels, that goal car, dream house, the ideal significant other, the career that paid the bills. I visualized it, worked hard for it, and got it. In my grasp, I had all those things I thought were success, that I thought would bring me continual happiness and fulfillment.

Until I realized that even though I had attained all these things I thought success represented, there was still a void, a loneliness, a longing for more. I continued to chase things. I'd get to the end of the race, and sure, for a moment there was pleasure and excitement for a job well done. But within minutes, or sometimes days, I'd feel empty again. I was never satisfied. I don't know about you, but when I go unsatisfied, for example, from not eating for an extended period of time, I start to get what we refer to in the fitness industry as "hangry," a combination of hungry and angry. It's what happens when you prolong eating when your body needs the fuel to keep you operating at your peak. You say things that you don't mean, and you act in ways that are not becoming of your best self. Trust me, it's not cute.

Just when I thought I had won, when I thought I had all I wanted, I realized that although I'd been successful in many areas of my life, I still had a feeling of lack or unfulfillment.

A lot of us are in search of success, and we think we've "arrived." Even after winning that World Champion title, we're still left feeling empty. Now granted, for a moment, you soak in all the glory of the big win… until you get home. Then it's quiet again, and once more you're left asking yourself, "Is this it?" This happens because what we're in search of is so much more than success. What we're actually trying to find is *significance.*

Significance is not found in the outcome. It's found in the *moment,* meaning we get to find the joy in the everyday moments that are given to us. It's the joy in maximizing our gifts, talents, and skills; the "being who we're created to be" that brings fulfillment. However, so many of us get lost in the race to the title that we forget to be present and grateful for exactly where we're at in that moment. That moment is where the gift, the significance, and the joy is found. That is success.

What value are you directly providing in correlation to the gifts and superpowers you've been given? So much of my world changed when my search for success switched to searching for significance. It was no longer about me. It turned into what could be done *through me* for others. Once I learned to let go of what I thought was my dream and started to chase after my potential to become who I was meant to be, my purpose started to flow, and following closely behind was joy.

I spent the majority of my adulthood looking for partners or results to define who I was. My fulfillment was directly connected to who or what could make me happy. Some people get married because they think they have found their "other half." Only later do they realize that neither of them was whole to begin with. And I'm sorry, but two halves don't equal a whole when it comes to a relationship. You must be whole and happy with who you are as an individual to start with. Another person cannot fill that void and make you happy. Yes, you can share moments that bring joy and happiness together. But there will always be an emptiness if you're not whole yourself first, nor understand what wholeness is.

Likewise, you will attract what you are. For a long time, I attracted "half" people who looked for happiness in outside sources because they weren't whole, just like I was back then. Emptiness festered in these relationships along with self-inflicted doubt and depression.

When you think you have won, you have just begun. Operating at champion level requires continuous challenges, reflection, and growth. It requires the surrender of ego. Operating at champion level feeds off service to others from a place of selflessness.

I have briefly touched on the challenges I've had with my oldest daughter. I've also touched on the challenges I had with my mother. The biggest drive behind my alter ego, "the Machine," was the desire to provide more for my kids and to put an end to the generational curse.

Sitting at my grandmother's funeral next to my brother and uncles, tears running down my face, I listened as her sons, my uncles, expressed the challenges my grandmother had faced as a mother and wife married to my grandfather. This was the first time I had heard these stories. Tears continued to fall down my face as I listened to what seemed all too familiar to me. I also heard of her strength and determination to make a better life for her family. She sounded so much like my mother, and some of the battles they both faced seemed eerily familiar. The entire situation brought flashbacks of my mother's funeral fifteen years prior. The pain. The generational curse was all too present... still. The fight for a better life was passed on to me; it was now in my hands to recreate our family lineage.

Just as I have shared in this book with you, I quickly activated my fighter stance and chose to fight. In and out of relationships where I'd battled so many insecurities, failures, and lost hope, I decided to put an end to it. I'd no longer operate at a level unequal to my true identity. I am whole, capable, and worthy. From that day forward, I fully surrendered to my authentic self, the woman God created me to be, and to my mission to end this generational cycle that many women face, continue to repeat, and suffer in with their families.

What does it mean to fully surrender? It means that we no longer operate from a place of fear or ego, but from a place of expectancy. This is based on the foundation of faith that the Most High God loves us more than anything, despite what we believe to be our shortcomings. That we're whole, always have been whole, but somehow, somewhere, we let society, labels, or ego break us down. We're meant to be champions. We're meant to have that title. To hold this title, we must continue to surrender every day to our toughest opponent: the ego. And we will be tested every day; this is just how it works.

Faith Untested Cannot Be Trusted

Just when I thought I had surrendered it all, I was tested. My daughter, Kat, secretly FaceTimed me. All I could see was her huddled on the floor against a wall, but I could hear "Jake," her boyfriend, shouting obscenities. Jake then declared, "I am not going to let you leave here alive! You belong to me!" He was clearly high on some drug. I could see she was in a hostage situation with him in their apartment. She desperately needed my help.

The time was 7:30 a.m., and this was really happening. I knew I needed to act. Now. Despite how I was feeling and the conflicts in my head about our troublesome past, unconditional love and the desire to protect my daughter trumped any ego trying to push its way through that was telling me *Leave her to work this out on her own.*

I arrived at her apartment after a twenty-minute drive while praying and crying out to God to protect her until I got there. Jake was aware she'd called me for help and had darted to the parking lot to intercept me. But he was greeted by a friend of mine I had called on the way, "Hammer," who kept him distracted while I searched for Kat.

When I rushed through the side door on the first floor of this three-story apartment complex, I was confronted by three men in their mid-twenties, who were Jake's "posse." They were strapped, and one had donned brass knuckles as they blocked the doorway. Their aggravated faces clearly indicated they weren't going to let me pass. But I had a job to do, and that was to protect my daughter. My faith was being tested. The question was, could I operate in faith, not in fear? Could I accomplish the mission?

There was no other option; my daughter's life was at stake. I flexed my muscles and shot them a look that clearly said, *You don't want to mess with me!* Then I pushed right through them and up the stairs to the second floor. I was like a general, heading into battle with the confidence of an entire army behind me.

I opened the door to her room and found Kat still huddled on the floor, somewhat in a daze. Above her head was a hole in the wall Jake had made with his fist. Flashbacks of a similar situation I went through, my mom went through, and her mom went through troubled my mind. But I knew what needed to be done.

We had a mission: "Operation Extraction" went into full speed. I helped my daughter to her feet, and we rapidly filled bags, grabbed her pets, and evacuated the apartment like the building was on fire. I guarded Kat with what could only be described as a "mother's love." I transported her back down the stairs and right through the phalanx of men whose scare tactics couldn't shake the power and protection of my faith.

My heart was aching for understanding. I worked so hard up until this point to prepare a life for my daughter that would be absent of such tragedy, to stop the generational curse of emotional and physical abuse. I had failed.

Or so I thought. What I realized that day, when I chose to take time to reflect, is that I had indeed stopped a generational curse. I was there for my daughter, with unconditional, selfless love, like I had wanted my mom to do for me. And I can only imagine my mom wanted her mom to do the same when she experienced similar battles. I had fully surrendered my ego. I was filled with faith, not fear. I had mastered letting go of what I thought I had to do and letting God work through me. I listened and obeyed that *still small voice.* The outcome was irrelevant; the generational curse I had been striving so hard to bring to an end became obsolete.

* * *

"Astonished, King Nebuchadnezzar stood up in terror and asked his advisors, 'Didn't we throw three men into the fire, bound firmly with ropes?'

In reply, they told the king, 'Yes, Your Majesty.'

'Look!' he told them, 'I see four men walking untied and unharmed in the middle of the fire, and the appearance of the fourth resembles a divine being.'

Then Nebuchadnezzar approached the opening of the blazing fire furnace. He shouted out, 'Shadrach, Meshach, and Abednego, servants of the Most High God, come out and come here!' So Shadrach, Meshach, and Abednego came out of the fire."

–Daniel 3:24-26 (ISV)

* * *

That's what operating as a champion is all about: letting go of self and surrendering to the Divine Plan. That day, not only did my faith get tested, but God's reckless, unrelenting, agape love for his children will forever be part of my testimony. *He* was the "fourth man in the fire" that day with us, guiding me and protecting us the entire time. That day God protected my daughter, me, and my selfless friend "Hammer" because of our faith.

* * *

Have you mastered finding peace and joy within yourself, and are you not dependent on outside sources or people? I would have been searching forever if I had continued to try to find happiness by putting an end to a generational curse. When you can finally let go and let God have full control, you will fully grasp your purpose. When you can continuously operate at a level of faith and are consistently in the pursuit of joy and oneness with who you're created to be, with confidence in yourself, your destiny will continue to unfold. Miracles will be performed through you like they were through me that day. And I've had so many miracles performed through me since that day. When we fully surrender, life is a series of miracles shaping our destiny until we finally return home. The joy is found in the journey and the pursuit to perform at your best with the gifts that have been endowed to you.

* * *

"His master replied, "Well done, good and faithful servant! You have been faithful with a few things; I'll put you in charge of many things. Come and share your master's happiness!" (Matthew 25:23, NIV)

* * *

The mission must continue, faithful servant. The work is the gift. Continue to be vigilant, and watch as you're rewarded with the opportunity to make an even greater impact. Just when you think you have won, you have just begun. The *impact* is the win.

ROUND 9 TAKEAWAYS

1. We GET to find the joy in the everyday moments that are given to us.
2. It's not about you; it's all about what can be done *through* you for others.
3. Operating at champion level requires continuous challenges, reflection, and growth. It requires the surrender of ego.
4. When you can finally let go and let God have full control, you will fully grasp your purpose.

Conclusion

THE FINAL BELL

"I have fought the good fight,
I have finished the race,
I have kept the faith."
–2 Timothy 4:7 (NIV)

When I look back on my journey, from the desert heat of Iraq to the battles I've fought on my knees, in business, in relationships, and in faith, I see the same truth written through them all. The fight was never meant to break me. It was meant to build me.

Every round mattered. Every hit shaped me. Every scar told a story of grace, grit, and growth.

If you've walked through these pages with me, you've done more than read words. You've trained. You've reflected. You've remembered who you are. And if you're holding this book, I need you to know this: You are ready for whatever comes next.

Your Corner Debrief

You've built your **F**oundation on faith.
You've learned to **I**gnite your purpose in the face of fear.
You've chosen to **G**et to work even when you didn't feel ready.
You've guarded your **H**eart, **H**ands, and **H**ead to stay in alignment.
And you've taken **T**ime to reflect, to learn, and to grow.

This isn't the end of your fight. It's the beginning of a new stance. You are no longer reacting to life; you are responding with divine authority. You've learned to transform adversity into your ally and to see your scars not as signs of defeat but as proof that you endured the fight.

The world doesn't need perfect people. It needs prepared ones.

You are prepared.

Declaration

THE CHAMPION'S CREED

I am a fighter.
I am built on faith, grounded in grace, and fueled by purpose.
I do not run from the battle; I rise within it.
I am disciplined, resilient, and ready.
I am not defined by what hit me, but by how I got back up.
I train daily in truth.
I fight with love.
I lead with courage.
I move in divine momentum.
I am not here just to win rounds; I am here to transform them.
My faith is my foundation.
My fight is my testimony.

When the world grows dark, I will be light.
When fear speaks, I will answer with faith.
When others fall, I will help them rise.
I will build fighters of faith, and walk with them toward victory.

I was born for this battle.
I was chosen for this mission.

And by the strength of God within me, I will fight the good fight, finish the race, and keep the faith.

So, fighter, take your stance. Lift your chin.
Your mission field is waiting.

You've trained for this moment.
Now go show the world what faith in motion looks like.

ACKNOWLEDGMENTS

First and always, **Abba Father**.
You are my foundation and the Author of my life. You ordered my steps, sustained me in unseen seasons, and used every trial for Your purpose. This book exists because You are faithful.

To **Jesus Christ**, my Savior and my Friend.
You met me in the hardest moments and stayed close when the cost was high. You transformed what was meant to break me into what built me. Every truth in these pages flows from grace, received through faith.

To the **Holy Spirit**.
My guide and strength. You sharpened my discernment and gave me the courage to keep standing when quitting would have been easier.

To my **children**.
You are my why and my witness. I love you deeply, and I am so proud of you. Every word was written with your future in mind. May you always know that faith is your foundation, and the fight you face can become your testimony when surrendered to God.

To those who **shaped me through the hard moments**.
Some walked with me.

Some wounded me.
All of it refined me.
What was painful, God used.
What was broken, Jesus redeemed.

To my **mentors and spiritual leaders**.
Thank you for helping me hold my stance when the pressure increased. Your wisdom, prayer, correction, and belief mattered more than you know.

To my **community and fellow fighters**.
We rise together. We fight together. Your courage, unity, love, and commitment gave language to this message. Thank you for locking arms with me in the fight.

Faith is my foundation.
The fight is my testimony.

"And we know that in all things God works for the good of those who love Him, who have been called according to His purpose."
–Romans 8:28

THANK YOU FOR READING MY BOOK!

As a thank you for buying this book, I'd love to connect!

Scan the QR Code:

I appreciate your interest in my book and value your feedback, as it helps me improve future versions. I would appreciate it if you could leave your invaluable review on Amazon.com with your feedback. Thank you!

www.ingramcontent.com/pod-product-compliance
Lightning Source LLC
LaVergne TN
LVHW010617100826
845148LV00014B/3001

* 9 7 9 8 9 0 1 5 8 0 6 8 4 *